SURRENDERING

THE SECRET

Healing the Heartbreak of

ABORTION

PICKING UP
THE PIECES

Published by LifeWay Press®
© 2008 • Pat Layton
Originally published as *Surrendering the Secret: Healing the Heartbreak of Abortion. Revised 2008.*

ISBN: 9781574943320
Item 005123170

This book is the text for course CG-1322 in the subject area
Personal Life \ Bible Studies in the Christian Growth Study Plan.

To order additional copies of this resource: write LifeWay Church Resources Customer Service; One LifeWay Plaza; Nashville, TN 37234-0113; FAX order to (615) 251-5933; call toll free (800) 458-2772; e-mail *orderentry@lifeway.com;* order online at *www.lifeway.com* or *www.SerendipityHouse.com;* or visit the LifeWay Christian Store serving you.

1-800-525-9563
www.SerendipityHouse.com

Printed in the United States of America

CONTENTS

LEADER RESOURCES

A Note from Pat

Welcome to *Surrendering the Secret!* Some Bible studies allow God to open doors of our hearts and invite Him in to do a supernatural work in our lives. Other studies squeeze us in some areas that God wants to refine in our lives. Still other studies allow us to nestle into God's gentle arms and just rest in His goodness and promises. *Surrendering the Secret* will take you into all three of these places.

I strongly encourage you to work through this healing journey with a small-group or, at the very least, to reach out to at least one other Christian woman you trust to walk with you. This is one of those tender walks that is best shared with someone you can lean on. You will be encouraged and supported as you allow God into rooms of your heart that might have been sealed for so long that a rusty lock secures them. You may have kept your secret for so long that you don't remember the details yourself. God remembers. He wants to set you free. He wants to shine a light on the ways that your abortion has kept you trapped in secrets, shadows, and shame. As you risk looking into your past, evaluating your present, and envisioning your future, you will discover wounds and barriers in your life that you didn't even know existed. You'll also awaken new desires and possibilities.

Let me be the first to grasp your hand, look you in the eye and say, "I understand. I have felt what you feel. I have been where you are. And I know that you don't have to settle for just surviving—you can truly live!"

You are special to me, and you are beloved by God. His heart's desire is to walk this healing and life-giving journey with you. You've been in the wilderness of secrets, despair, shadows, and shame long enough. It's time to heal. It's time to live the adventure, one that is much like a mountain climb, that God planned for you from the beginning. All you need is to be willing. He will map out your path, He will provide the shade and the water, and, when we get to the top our mountain, He will provide clear skies, crisp cool air, and a brand new view of our future.

You've been given incredible power—the choice to make life and the choice to take life. In picking up *Surrendering the Secret* you've made the choice to make life—to begin the journey toward healing and life rather than allowing your life and dreams to die with a past mistake. I can't wait to see what awesome things God will do in and through you.

Let's do this thing together!

In His Grip—

Surrendering the Secret
Healing the Heartbreak of Abortion

Without question, abortion can be one of the most traumatic experiences in a person's life. Research indicates that more than 40% of women of child-bearing age have experienced the pain of abortion. With these large numbers, that group could include your sisters, mothers, wives, friends, or even you. Many women hide the secret of abortion deep in their hearts, and they are suffering severe consequences. They carry an incredible burden while wearing smiles on their faces.

Over the years post-abortive women learn to live in silence and secrecy, stockpiling hurts they have buried deep inside. Many struggle for years with repressed memories, guilt, shame, and depression. Most women feel they are not allowed to talk about their abortion experiences because it was their "choice." They carry a great burden of shame and failure, afraid to reveal their hidden pain. Secrecy and shame are a destructive combination as women are forced to endure long-lasting destructive effects in isolation.

As with any traumatic experience, many post-abortive women experience physical, emotional, and spiritual symptoms related to post-abortion trauma. They may not even realize that their symptoms are directly related to a past abortion. Often the medical community overlooks abortion as a risk factor in a woman's physical and emotional health.

Find the path to healing through honest, interactive Bible study; meaningful group experiences; unique journaling exercises; and caring community. Pat Layton, founder and president of A Woman's Place Ministries and a speaker and trainer for several national organizations, knows first-hand from her own healing journey how devastating abortion can be. With more than 20 years of experience in guiding women to healing, the process in *Surrendering the Secret* has been proven effective time and time again.

Healing occurs best in the context of a redemptive community. As you join in a supportive and confidential environment with a small group of women who share abortion in their pasts, healing and restoration will come. On the journey to healing, you will find a renewed sense of hope and purpose for the future.

IMPORTANT NOTE: We strongly encourage you to connect with a small group of women with whom you can take this healing journey. The process in *Surrendering the Secret* is not one you should go through alone. At the very least, find one other woman who would agree to be a partner with you as you walk through this study. You can adapt many of the group activities if you have a partner.

Pat's Journal Entry 1

Each tick of the clock seemed like an hour as I stared at the door to the clinic. Abortion had been legal for years so the clinic boldly advertised the service I needed: "Termination of Pregnancy."

The emotions and forces that lead a woman to an abortion clinic are not easily buried or forgotten. Like constant, dependable companions, disillusionment, confusion, anger, pride, fear, rebellion, control, and shame stayed with me through the process and for years afterward.

It was late summer in Florida, and at 23 I was engaged to be married in a few weeks. My fiancé didn't know I was at the clinic. How could I tell him? He was my knight in shining armor who had come into my life to rescue me from years of bad relationship choices and a lifelong search for significance and value.

I was not about to jump off the back of my knight's white horse and walk off into the sunset … alone and pregnant. Abortion was my only hope. It had to be the right thing to do! I couldn't bear to admit one more failure to my family. And the two men in my life now deserved better from me. My five-year-old son was the only good thing I had to show for myself at that point, and my fiancé really had no idea what he'd gotten himself into.

Too much power for a young, insecure woman—the power to make life and to take life. I made the choice I thought would fix everything for everyone, especially for me.

The inviting Yellow Page™ ad and the reassuring nurse at the desk affirmed my choice with the promise that this would only take a few minutes. Within a few hours, I'd forget it ever happened. Oh, that it had been anything like a simple solution …

So here I am years later, stepping back into my past again, staring one more time at the entrance to the dilapidated old clinic. This time, though, I'm flooded with gratitude, joy, and peace as I recall all that God has done in my life over these past years. He's rescued me from despair and shame, transforming the messes of my life into a beautiful ministry of grace and healing. My life has meaning as I share my story of redemption with so many others who are deeply wounded by their secrets and shadows. God has restored my marriage and brought my entire family into His salvation.

I could never have imagined that walking back through the pain into my secrets and shadows would begin a healing journey that has led to such a wonderful place of intimacy with God and fullness of life!

WHERE HAVE YOU COME FROM?

BREAKING THE ICE

LEADER: *Read the introductory material, the leader's notes at the end of this book, and the separate Leader Guide (ISBN 9781415864692) available through LifeWay.com, SerendipityHouse. com or LifeWay Christian stores. The guide will equip you with a variety of ideas and supplemental information to support your group healing progress. View the video for session 1 (optional). "Breaking the Ice" questions are designed to help put people at ease and get them talking.*

1. Take some time to think about your childhood dream for your future. What did you think your life would be like?

2. How do you keep the photos from your past? Do you organize them or keep them randomly piled in boxes? Regardless of how we store them, why do you think photos are so valuable to us?

3. Have you ever lost or misplaced something of great value to you? How did you approach your search to find it?

Remembering the Past

Strolling down memory lane can be wonderful. Memories come and go when we least expect them. The smell of warm bakery bread propels us back to Grandma's house and we're eight years old again. Returning for a hometown high school reunion motivates us to drive up and down streets pointing out our elementary school, a dear friend's home, or our favorite burger hangout to a bored spouse or friend. In the same way, bad memories—even when we try so hard to suppress them—roll in and out of our minds and hearts on a daily basis, bringing pain instead of happiness.

For those of us going though *Surrendering the Secret*, memories of a past abortion are are seared deeply into our hearts and souls. We're about to embark on this new journey together—a journey to healing, freedom, acceptance, and hope on the other side of our pain.. There will be times when the journey doesn't seem to be very healing, but often we must go down before we go up and go back before we can go forward. If you'll trust the process, you'll see God working. When you look back on your life, you can see God's hand in many places where, at the time, you had no idea He was working for you. This is another one of those times. God is here, and He has brought you here. He has a plan for you but cannot take the journey for you. You must take one step: a step of faith to begin walking the path with Him.

Opening Prayer

God, thank You for Your supernatural ways and for leading me to this group. I know that You have another great work to do in me. You have known and cared for me since before I was born. I am thankful that I don't have to continue to carry this burden alone because You have promised to take this journey with me. I know, Lord, that many women are suffering just as I am with this secret. Help me, Lord, to know how You can use this in my life.

Objectives for This Session
- Grasp the importance of intentional healing from a past abortion
- Discover God's heart toward you and His desire for your healing
- Realize the need to go back to move ahead
- Prepare to move forward on a healing journey

DISCOVERING THE TRUTH

HEALING RATHER THAN BAND-AIDS

Almost everybody has experienced past trouble or trauma that has left deep heart wounds. Trouble and wounds are inevitable, but we have the power to choose how we'll deal with them.

There are many ways to "numb out" as we try to escape our pain or seek pleasure in a harsh world. Most of us think God couldn't care less about our pain or that He condemns us for past mistakes, but the Book of Jeremiah gives us a glimpse into God's real heart:

They dress the wound of my people as though it is not serious. "Peace, peace," they say, when there is not peace.
JEREMIAH 6:14, NIV

1. God was clearly critical of the religious leaders He's addressing. What attitudes toward people's pain and struggles was God criticizing? (Reread the verse.) When God looks at the messes in our lives, how does He feel about us and about our past wounds?

2. Rather than trying to ignore issues from our past, what might happen if we choose to intentionally remember the past and understand more about that day, that choice, when life changed forever?

3. How do you think this approach of remembering might be a more effective approach to finding inner healing and a richer life? In what ways would it be more difficult?

God knows superficial healing is no healing at all. True peace will not come until we experience true healing. Let's look at a story in the Bible about a woman, not so different than us, to see how true healing can come.

One Woman's Journey Backward

The Bible overflows with stories of women—their losses, challenges, good and bad choices, failures, and victories. The common themes and promises of God's Word are rescue, healing, redemption, and hope. Through these stories God promises never to ignore us, forsake us, or give up on us. Hagar is a woman in the Bible whose dream for family and motherhood didn't go the way she planned—the way she'd dreamed about since girlhood.

¹ Abram's wife Sarai had not borne him children. She owned an Egyptian slave named Hagar. ² Sarai said to Abram, "Since the Lord has prevented me from bearing children, go to my slave; perhaps I can have children by her." And Abram agreed to what Sarai said. ³ So Abram's wife Sarai took Hagar, her Egyptian slave, and gave her to her husband Abram as a wife for him. ... ⁴ He slept with Hagar, and she became pregnant. When she realized that she was pregnant, she looked down on her mistress. ⁵ Then Sarai said to Abram, "You are responsible for my suffering! I put my slave in your arms, and ever since she saw that she was pregnant, she has looked down on me. May the Lord judge between me and you." ⁶ Abram replied to Sarai, "Here, your slave is in your hands; do whatever you want with her." Then Sarai mistreated her so much that she ran away from her.

GENESIS 16:1-3,4-6, HCSB

LEADER: *Discuss as many discovery questions as time permits. Highlight in advance the questions you don't want to miss.*

4. What part of Abram and Sarai's issues became Hagar's (verses 4,6)? How do you feel about what happened to Hagar in this story?

5. Surely Hagar's decision to run away from her home and life was one of panic (verse 6). How must Hagar have felt about her circumstances, herself, and those she should have been able to trust? What kind of life could she expect with the problems she had and the choices she'd made?

7 The angel of the LORD found Hagar beside a spring of water in the wilderness, along the road to Shur. 8 The angel said to her, "Hagar, Sarai's servant, where have you come from, and where are you going?" "I'm running away from my mistress, Sarai," she replied.

9 The angel of the LORD said to her, "Return to your mistress, and submit to her authority." 10 Then he added, "I will give you more descendants than you can count." 11 And the angel also said, "You are now pregnant and will give birth to a son. You are to name him Ishmael (which means 'God hears'), for the LORD has heard your cry of distress. ... 13 Thereafter, Hagar used another name to refer to the LORD, who had spoken to her. She said, "You are the God who sees me." She also said, "Have I truly seen the One who sees me?" 14 So that well was named Beer-lahai-roi (which means "well of the Living One who sees me"). It can still be found between Kadesh and Bered. 15 So Hagar gave Abram a son, and Abram named him Ishmael.

GENESIS 16:7-11,13-15, NLT

6. Hagar and her unborn son were going to die in the wilderness, but Hagar turned to God in her time of crisis. What was His first instruction to her through the angel (verse 9)? Why did the angel instruct her to name her unborn son *Ishmael* (verse 11)?

7. It was common in biblical times for people to give God a new name when they discovered another exciting characteristic about Him. Given the way Hagar named God and the place where He met her, what fresh, life-sustaining truths do you think Hagar learned about God and the way He related to her personally?

A Response of Panic, A Life of Secrets

For thousands of women every day, abortion is a response to panic. While abortion promises to be the simple solution to the problem of an unwanted or unexpected pregnancy, it doesn't solve all our problems and it creates new problems for us. Sooner or later, we run to the wilderness of fear, shame, abandonment, anger, and self-protection only to find ourselves just surviving—not really living—in a foreign, desolate land.

8. Describe a time in your life, apart from your abortion, when you tried to run from a problem or tried to slide out of your situation without anyone noticing. How did it work out?

The amazing news is that God longs to come to us and rescue us. When God found Hagar feeling abandoned and hopeless in the wilderness, she embraced her pain rather than trying to cover it up or ignore it. You may feel as though you've been wandering in a desert since your abortion experience, ever aware of your losses. Or you may have made a futile decision long ago to try to put that desert experience behind you, to bury it and try to disconnect your heart and life from it. God hears your heart's cry! He sees you and feels your pain. He longs for you to look back on this time in your life and ask with Hagar, "Have I truly seen the One who sees me?"

Our heart's desire is that this *Surrendering the Secret* study will be your angel in the desert, walking with you back to face the secrets, shadows, and shame that have kept you from really living for too long. As difficult and scary as it might be, you must confront your pain head on. Just like Hagar, you have a promise that God will meet you personally at your place of need.

EMBRACING THE TRUTH

GOD SEARCHES FOR THOSE WHO ARE LOST

Often the greatest obstacle to healing is our own resistance to the journey. There are many reasons to hold back, but one with which most of us struggle is doubting God's heart toward us. Given the pain and struggles in our lives, it's no wonder we ask ourselves, "If God is good, how could He have let this happen to me?" It's also understandable, given the way most of us have been raised, that we focus on God's judgment and greatly underestimate His incredible desire and passion for each of us. Let's consider His words to us.

[17] For God did not send his Son into the world to condemn the world, but to save the world through him ... [21] But whoever lives by the truth comes into the light, so that it may be seen plainly that what he has done has been done through God.

JOHN 3:17,21, NIV

[12] As a shepherd looks after his scattered flock when he is with them, so will I look after my sheep. I will rescue them from all the places where they were scattered on a day of clouds and darkness. ... [15] I myself will tend my sheep and have them lie down, declares the Sovereign LORD. [16] I will search for the lost and bring back the strays. I will bind up the injured and strengthen the weak.

EZEKIEL 34:12,15-16, NIV

[Jesus responded to the grumbling of religious leaders about his hanging out with "sinners" with this story:] [4] "Suppose one of you had a hundred sheep and lost one. Wouldn't you leave the ninety-nine in the wilderness and go after the lost one until you found it? [5] When found, you can be sure you would put it across your shoulders, rejoicing, [6] and when you got home call in your friends and neighbors, saying, 'Celebrate with me! I've found my lost sheep!' [7] Count on it—there's more joy in heaven over one sinner's rescued life than over ninety-nine good people in no need of rescue."

LUKE 15:4-7, THE MESSAGE

1. According to John 3:17-21, what was God's desire and goal for sending Jesus into our world? Have you ever considered that God is devoted to a save and rescue mission for our messed up world and for you in particular? How does this truth change your perspective?

2. Face it, sheep aren't too bright, and they clearly can't protect themselves. According to Ezekiel 34:12,15-16, how does God deal with us when we get lost in the fog or darkness of life? How does God's promise apply to our own life issues, wounds, addictions, and spiritual struggles?

3. From His story in Luke 15, what is Jesus' approach to leading and caring for you as one of His sheep? How does the way He values and even treasures you personally affect your willingness to be "found" by Him?

Our Relentless Lover

God uses many metaphors to communicate the depth of His feelings for us—from shepherd-sheep, to potter-clay, to father-child, and even lover-beloved. The metaphor of lover to beloved best expresses the depth of intimacy He longs for with each of us.

⁴ Long before [God] laid down earth's foundations, he had us in mind, had settled on us as the focus of his love, to be made whole and holy by his love. ⁵ Long, long ago he decided to adopt us into his family through Jesus Christ. (What pleasure he took in planning this!) ⁶ He wanted us to enter into the celebration of his lavish gift-giving by the hand of his beloved Son. ⁷ Because of the sacrifice of the Messiah, his blood poured out on the altar of the Cross, we're a free people—free of penalties and punishments chalked up by all our misdeeds. And not just barely free, either. Abundantly free!

EPHESIANS 1:4-7, THE MESSAGE

As a bridegroom rejoices over his bride, so will your God rejoice over you.

ISAIAH 62:5, NIV

² When you're in over your head, I'll be there with you. When you're in rough waters, you will not go down. When you're between a rock and a hard place, it won't be a dead end—³ Because I am God, your personal God, The Holy of Israel, your Savior. I paid a huge price for you: all of Egypt, with rich Cush and Seba thrown in! ⁴ That's how much you mean to me! That's how much I love you! I'd sell off the whole world to get you back, trade the creation just for you.

ISAIAH 43:2-4, THE MESSAGE

4. What does it mean to be the "focus" of someone's love (Ephesians 1:4)? How does a bridegroom feel about his new bride (Isaiah 62:5)?

5. As a bride, how would it feel if your lover would give away everything in exchange for your love (Isaiah. 43:4)?

6. What other phrases in Ephesians 1:4-7 and Isaiah 43:2-4 explain the depth of God's desire for a deep, personal relationship with you?

7. In what ways is a good husband-wife relationship more intimate and joy-filled than any other human relationship? What does the lover-bride image tell us about the depth of intimacy and joy for which God created us?

God is *thrilled* about *you*, and longs to see you enthused about a freer and deeper life with Him. All too often, we fall into a pattern of "lookin' for love in all the wrong places" rather than turning to God to meet our deepest needs for intimacy, acceptance, and meaning. God is a relentless lover, but He's also a gentle lover. He wants you to rest in His arms, comforted in those times when you're lost, trapped, or struggling. Take comfort in knowing that even in those dark places, He's still coming for you!

CONNECTING

Surrendering the Secret will walk with you through some secrets that have been stored away in your heart but not forgotten. It will help you cope with memories of bad choices that drop into your heart and mind when you least expect them. Remember, God has a way of taking us backward to take us forward and inward to take us outward.

MY WILDERNESS

The wilderness we wander is not a literal desert; it's a wilderness of our hearts and minds. When we carry a heavy burden, it's only natural to feel trapped by the shadows that surround us. Like Hagar, we grow weary and feel ready to give up in despair and shame.

As if that weren't enough, there's a villain in the story who always follows us into the wilderness. Instead of seeing the "God who sees me" and who works tirelessly on our behalf, we hear the inner voices of condemnation and shame ... and the lying voice of the tempter.

1. Take a few moments to read each statement in the following survey and mark the appropriate answers:

Past Trauma Survey

	Yes	No	Not Sure
1. The abortion happened over a year ago.	☐	☐	☐
2. I do not know the name of the doctor who performed it.	☐	☐	☐
3. I was more than three months pregnant when I aborted.	☐	☐	☐
4. I was a teenager at the time of the abortion.	☐	☐	☐
5. I was forced by others to abort.	☐	☐	☐
6. The baby's father wanted me to abort.	☐	☐	☐
7. The baby's father left the decision up to me.	☐	☐	☐
8. Less than six people know about the abortion.	☐	☐	☐
9. I always felt abortion was wrong but had no choice in my situation.	☐	☐	☐
10. I have experienced nightmares or flashbacks about the abortion.	☐	☐	☐
11. Nightmares or flashbacks occur at least once each month.	☐	☐	☐
12. There are details about the abortion that I cannot remember.	☐	☐	☐
13. I avoid places, people, and things that remind me of the abortion.	☐	☐	☐
14. I fear that my life may be short.	☐	☐	☐
15. Since the abortion, I have lost interest in things I used to love.	☐	☐	☐
16. I often have trouble sleeping.	☐	☐	☐
17. I often feel angry and irritable.	☐	☐	☐
18. Concentrating is often difficult.	☐	☐	☐
19. I feel guilt and shame about the abortion.	☐	☐	☐
20. I have cried over the abortion.	☐	☐	☐
21. I use alcohol and/or drugs at least once per week.	☐	☐	☐
22. I usually have sex with the men I date.	☐	☐	☐
23. Sometimes I regret having the abortion.	☐	☐	☐
24. I feel sad and depressed often.	☐	☐	☐
25. I had physical problems after the abortion.	☐	☐	☐
26 I feel bad emotionally from the abortion at times.	☐	☐	☐
27. I feel that I made the right decision to abort.	☐	☐	☐
28. I feel OK about the whole experience.	☐	☐	☐
29. I would abort again to deal with an unplanned pregnancy.	☐	☐	☐
30. I have had more than one abortion.	☐	☐	☐

TOTALS: _____ _____ _____

Survey Interpretation: If the number of checks in your "yes" column is 9 or more, post-abortion trauma is probably already affecting your life. If the number is higher than 14, you have numerous symptoms that need attention. If you answered, "yes" to 5 or more questions in numbers 10-18, you may be struggling with post-traumatic stress disorder (PTSD) resulting from your abortion or some other trauma in your life.

2. Share with the group or your prayer partner your overall survey score and key symptoms you recognize in your own life, even if you don't directly associate these symptoms with your abortion(s).

3. Were you surprised by the connection between any of the symptoms in the survey and the condition that medical and counseling professionals refer to as Post-Abortion Trauma? Explain.

If you are working on this study alone, I encourage you again to ask a close Christian friend or female ministry leader to work through this process with you. Post-Abortion Trauma is real and it is deep. You need someone who will pray with you, help you through this, and someone you can trust. God has someone for you; find her!

CHOICES

Most of us have learned to accommodate our past. We live with it, we ignore it, we justify it, we blame others for it, and we carry it into our fears, attitudes, and relationships.

There are choices given to every woman—the choice to make life and the choice to take life. We exercised that choice in going though with an abortion, but more importantly we exercise it now. Will you take the journey to healing and life, or will you allow your life and dreams to die with a past mistake?

Remember, God is with you. If you've chosen to take this journey on your own, He is with you. If you have chosen a partner or friend to help you, He is with you. If you are taking your journey with a group, He is with you. You matter to God! He wants you whole, He wants you healed, He wants you free!

²³ *A [woman's] steps are established by the* LORD, *and He takes pleasure in [her] way.* ²⁴ *Though [she] falls, [she] will not be overwhelmed, because the* LORD *holds [her] hand.*

PSALM 37:23-24, HCSB
(FEMININE PRONOUNS ADDED FOR EMPHASIS)

MY HEALING JOURNEY

WHERE HAVE YOU COME FROM?

As we close this session, we'll review the journey that God takes us on to bring about our healing. Together we'll take the first vital step.

LEADER: *For unique and meaningful group experience ideas, refer to the separate Leader Guide. (For continued support please go to www.surrenderingthesecret.com or www.surrenderingthesecret.blogspot.com.)*

YOU ARE NOT ALONE

Think of our next couple of months together as a challenging mountain trek. It's time to confront our fear and pain and begin the slow, steady journey to the summit. It takes faith and courage to tackle this mountain. We're going together because the view from the top is worth the struggle, pain, and sacrifices on the journey upward.

This healing journey through *Surrendering the Secret* will help you to get to the summit. There the stigma of abortion is gone, there is personal healing, we enjoy reconciliation with God and our unborn children, and we find a life of secrets, shame, and shadows completely redeemed!

If you are not part of a healing group, decide today whom you will trust to walk this journey with you. If you are, pray for the other members in your group. They are just as afraid and ashamed as you are. Ask God to help you help one another.

What is your greatest need for prayer and practical support right now? Record in the following space your greatest prayer and support needs and then those of your prayer partner or group.

My Prayer and Support Needs

My Group's Prayer and Support Needs

Taking Truth Home

Each week "Taking Truth Home" section will contain an introspective question to ask of your heart or a question to take to God. There may also be journaling or other activities to help you in your healing process. Some journal pages are included in the member book; however, journaling is a powerful tool to accelerate healing and spiritual growth. You may want to begin a separate journal during this healing journey and continue it on your walk with God.

This part of your study will help you to look into your heart and into God's heart as you move closer to Him with the deepest and darkest places of your soul. This first week the "Taking Truth Home" assignment will be challenging, but it is vital to our journey together. There are two elements this week—questions to take to your heart about the lies we believe and a time to journal of your abortion experience.

Questions to Take to My Heart
The following questions ask you to look into your heart and focus on your deepest feelings about yourself and God. Our behaviors are the best indicators of what we really believe deep down. Look deep into the underlying beliefs in your heart where your truest

attitudes and motives live. To prepare yourself, read Psalm 51:6 and spend time reflecting. Don't settle for a quick answer. Be sure to capture your thoughts.

✳ Which of these lies has the tempter whispered in my ear about myself, my secret, my relationships?

❏ Need—Burying secrets and shame and keeping my pride are critical to my survival.
❏ Fear—I won't be able to cope without my secrets and coping mechanisms.
❏ Inferiority—I'm a bad, unworthy person. Nobody could really like me.
❏ Isolation—I'm all alone anyway, so it's up to me to take care of me.
❏ Failure—I'm a failure anyway, so why even try?
❏ Shame—My behaviors and addictions are the truest things about me.
❏ Self-hatred—I should loathe myself for who I am and what I've done.
❏ Escape—I must find a way to avoid the pain and isolation.
❏ Disillusionment: There's no hope. No one could understand or love me.
❏ Other: _____ .

✳ Which of these lies has the tempter whispered in my ear about God? Which false belief about God is my biggest obstacle in the journey to healing? What do I really believe about God's heart toward me?

❏ God only puts up with me at best; He doesn't really love and delight in me.
❏ God can't be trusted to have my best interests at heart.
❏ God is demanding; He's only satisfied with perfection.
❏ God really doesn't care; He's abandoned me.
❏ God doesn't want "damaged goods."
❏ Maybe this whole God thing is a sham.
❏ God only helps those who help themselves.
❏ Other: _____

✳ Are there particular times or situations in which you're more susceptible to the inner voices of shame and the Devil's lies? Explain or give an example.

Journal Exercise

In session 2 we'll take the first step at looking honestly at Post-Abortion Trauma and how it may have or is currently affecting your life. We'll dig into the truth about physical, social, emotional, and spiritual aspects of abortion. Every woman who has chosen abortion as a way of escape has been sold a lie. Lies create secrecy, bondage, darkness, and shame. God wants to set you free, but you will have to fight for your freedom through a sometimes uncomfortable journey.

Two common lies we buy are that our stories are worse than anybody else's and that we should have known better than to let our lives take such turns in the first place. We must remember that these self-centered lies feed our pride and will hinder the healing process. We must let go of our pride and be honest with ourselves about our pasts in order to avoid staying stuck there.

In the space provided or in your personal journal, write down events that led up to your abortion. Describe the events of the day and write down what you remember thinking and feeling during that time in your life. Raw thoughts and fragmented sentences are fine; the key is to get your story on paper. Some questions you might consider follow on page 24.

My Abortion Experience

My Abortion Experience

Questions to Consider for Your Abortion Journal

1. How old were you when you had your first abortion?

2. What was your lifestyle at the time of your abortion?

3. Were you making poor choices in relationships with men?

4. What was your relationship with your parents?

5. Was there anyone in your life you felt you could trust completely?

6. What was your relationship with God?

7. How did you view abortion at the time (for example, right, wrong, OK for some but not for me)?

8. When you discovered you were pregnant, what was your first thought?

9. Did you tell anyone about your pregnancy?

10. What emotions tended to overwhelm you as you thought about the pregnancy?

11. When did the idea of abortion first enter your mind? Was it suggested to you by someone?

12. Did you feel you "had no other choice" in the situation? What circumstances made you feel this way?

13. Did anyone offer support for the pregnancy?

14. How did you find the abortion facility?

15. Did you go alone or did someone take you to the abortion appointment?

16. When you first arrived at the clinic, how did you feel? (Some women report that they continued to hope that someone might rescue them.)

17. When you first entered the clinic, what did you see, hear, and feel?

18. What do you remember about the abortion procedure?

19. While you were recovering, what thoughts were playing in your mind?

20. Were there any complications with your procedure?

21. Who took you home?

22. What about you changed the day of the abortion?

Surrendering the Secret Pledge

Whether you are going through this study with a group or a trusted friend, it is important that you covenant together, agreeing to live out important group values. Once these values are agreed upon, the group will be on its way to experiencing true redemptive community. It's very important that your group discuss these values early in the study. Your group leader will have a more detailed pledge that she will distribute.

1. I am committed and determined to go through this healing process, staying with the group until completion.

2. During this process I will not numb my feelings by using drugs or alcohol.

3. I will not consider suicide or make any type of self-destructive plan.

4. I understand that although this is a personal journey I have a responsibility to the group and its members.

5. I understand and agree that this is a closed group. What is shared in *The Healing Journey* stays in *The Healing Journey*, NO EXCEPTIONS.

6. I will do the homework that is assigned to me on a weekly basis in preparation for the next session.

7. I acknowledge that this will be hard work, confronting the loss associated with abortion and the effects on my life.

8. I trust that God wants me healed and set free.

_____   _____
         Signature   *Date*

Pat's Journal Entry 2

I couldn't imagine why God had brought me down this path in my healing journey. Why was He asking me to share my past? My heart was pounding and my head was spinning. My friend, Ann, with her sparkling smile, was bounding toward me from the tea room parking lot. No getting away this time! It was too late to duck. Ann instinctively reached for my hands as I began to tremble and tears ran down my cheeks. I had never been so scared in my life!

Ann was my new best friend. She first approached me at a church ladies' retreat. She had invested in me, pulling me into her circle of beautiful, godly women and coaching me in my new walk with God. It was Ann who taught me how to pray out loud. She was the one who planted within me a hunger for the Bible and a desire for intimacy with God. She continued to walk with me step-by-step through the metamorphosis into my new life in Jesus.

A little over a year had passed since I surrendered my life to God at that ladies' retreat. Within the year, my life had turned around so beautifully. My marriage, my children, even my music had been immersed in the new life Jesus offers, and my spirit and emotions were floating. Little did I suspect that this incredible walk into new life with God would lead me to a crossroads where I found myself face-to-face with a dark secret from my old life. Not only had I hidden this secret from the world, but I had also stuffed it so deeply inside that I was hiding it from myself.

As I clutched Ann's hands at the tea room, I felt like my newly found peace and joy was about to be demolished. But I knew that God was asking me to surrender my secret, just as He'd asked that I surrender my life to Him.

Although I was dreading it, I had to tell Ann about my abortion. The secret swelled so fiercely in my heart that I was about to burst! Yet turmoil and panic gripped my chest because I had no idea what Ann would say or how exposing this dark part of my past would affect our friendship. Ann and all my new friends at church seemed so godly and good. What would they think of me? What would they think about the awful thing I had done?

It was time—time to break the power of secrecy ...

SHARING THE SECRET
A SPRING IN THE DESERT

BREAKING THE ICE

LEADER: *These questions are designed to help group members get to know each other better. The more connected group members are, the more open and healing the group will become. Questions 4 and 5 invite sharing from the homework assignment. View the video for session 2 (optional).*

1. Recall some lines from nursery rhymes, songs, or fairy tales that adulthood has taught you are impossible. (Examples: "the cow jumped over the moon," "when you wish upon a star ... anything your heart desires will come to you," or concepts similar to Jack's beanstalk and Cinderella's pumpkin carriage.)

2. If you had to confess a childhood "sin"—something you never told your parents you did—what would you confess?

3. Share a lie or broken promise that changed your life (Santa Claus myth, boyfriend who pledged his love but left, and so forth).

4. Spend some time considering the things you learned in the first session. What thoughts or behaviors in your life may be connected to your past abortion? Have you ever considered the enemy might be involved? Explain.

5. Which false belief about God most plagues you? What past wounds might drive this belief?

OPENING PRAYER

Jesus, thank You for drawing me into this safe harbor where I have truth instead of judgment, grace instead of condemnation, and Your strength instead of my isolation. You know the pain I'm feeling. Hebrews 4:15 says that You've been tempted in every way as I have, but in Your divine power You overcame it all! Give me Your power, Your peace, and Your grace to press through this process. Let me feel Your presence today as together we break the power of secrecy.

OBJECTIVES FOR THIS SESSION

- Understand the dangers of silence and secrecy
- Review the enemy's scheme to wound us and keep us in bondage
- Realize that truth sets us free from the lies deeply embedded in our hearts
- Embrace the need to bring the shadows of secrecy into the "light"
- Break the power of secrecy by sharing our abortion experiences with someone we trust
- Begin to move from isolation into the healing environment of redemptive community

DISCOVERING THE TRUTH

In the first session, we talked a little about our power to make life and take life. We agreed to press on through this healing journey to find the freedom and peace God wants for us. Our focus in session 2 is breaking the power of silence and secrecy that has held us captive for too long.

MY HEALING JOURNEY

Sharing the Secret: A Spring in the Desert

Where Have You Come From?

SILENCE AND SECRECY

No one has to teach a child to lie—a fact pointing to an amazing phenomenon and a constant reminder that in our fallen world, deception is the norm rather than the exception.

1. What are some reasons children tell lies? How about adults?

Some people lie for their own selfish gain, but many lie to avoid exposure, loneliness, or vulnerability. Children learn quickly that lying can get them into trouble, so they either choose to be more truthful or resort to more lies, sneaking around, or clamming up in silence. What's amazing is that as adults, we continue in these same patterns. We all have secrets—things we've done we hope no one will ever know about.

²³ For everyone has sinned; we all fall short of God's glorious standard. ²⁴ Yet God, with undeserved kindness, declares that we are righteous. He did this through Christ Jesus when he freed us from the penalty for our sins.

ROMANS 3:23-24, NLT

2. According to Romans 3:23, who is exempt from sins, mistakes, and failures? If we know we've all sinned and fall short of God's glory, why do you think we so often resort to silence and secrets?

Every one of us hides something we don't want others to know about—something we're ashamed of. The villain in the story, the Devil, knows that as long as he can keep us bound by our silence and secrets, as long as he can keep us isolated and separated from others, he can keep us from the freedom God offers us.

Buying into Lies

Over the years, as we learn to live in silence and secrecy, many of us end up with a large stockpile of hurts that we've buried deep inside ourselves. To live free of those hurts, we must learn to recognize the lies we've accepted as truths and begin to speak the truth to ourselves. Lies about yourself, God, other people, and the world in which we live will keep you trapped in old wounds and unhealthy ways of living. Culture bombards us with myths and deceptions about sex, love, and life. That's why Jesus spoke strongly about the deceiver who plants so many lies in our world and in our hearts.

The devil ... was a murderer from the beginning, not holding to the truth, for there is no truth in him. When he lies, he speaks his native language, for he is a liar and the father of lies.

JOHN 8:44, NIV

Be sober! Be on the alert! Your adversary the Devil is prowling around like a roaring lion, looking for anyone he can devour.

1 PETER 5:8, HCSB

3. What was Jesus' attitude toward the villain in the larger story and in our personal stories? How did He describe the Devil's nature, intentions, and strategies in John 8:44?

4. What did Jesus identify as the native language of the Devil? What did He indicate happens to us when we believe the lies of the deceiver? (See also 1 Peter 5:8.)

The Devil's goal is to isolate you and take you out. He is the master deceiver. He encourages our tendency to try to escape. He doesn't want us to remember our wounds and stay in our pain until we figure out the path to healing and living large. Unwilling to face our intense emotions or to take responsibility about where we go from here, we let our burdens become our identities and we settle for survival in place of real life.

Leader: Review the following "Captive Heart Model" developed by author Ron Keck. Read the explanations in this section Each person's journey and role in the larger story is unique. Only God has all the answers. Involve group members by asking volunteers to read.

We all experience pain and choose many methods to try to escape it: We ignore our problems, turn to drugs or alcohol, or even sink into depression. When tempted to fall back into our old ruts, we're wise to remember that the enemy strategically shoots arrows or uses the wounds in our lives to distort our perception of who we are. If he can keep us feeling worthless, keep us feeling guilty, or keep our minds and hearts under his influence, he can keep us out of the glory God intended us to live in and the intimacy God wants us to share with Him. That's why the deceiver continually whispers lies about who we are, who God is, God's heart toward us, and intimacy with God.

Author Ron Keck developed the following model to describe the process of our hearts being captured and enslaved by the Devil. By better understanding his methods, we're better prepared to avoid the Devil's traps.

WOUNDS	• Strategic ARROWS are launched into our lives to create WOUNDS: A difficult loss ... painful circumstances ... a traumatic event ... neglect ... abuse
LIES	• Our WOUNDS become infected with LIES or false beliefs: "God has abandoned me too." ... "I'm a failure." ... "Nobody cares; it's up to me to look out for me."
AGREEMENTS	• Satan repeats LIES until we make AGREEMENTS to accept them as truth: "I'm on my own now." ... "There's no hope." ... I can't live without it." ... "This is all I deserve."
VOWS	• Once AGREEMENTS are made, VOWS are soon to follow: "I will never again ..." "From now on, I will always ..."
FALSE SELF	• False agreements and vows feed the FALSE SELF: Our distorted views about who we are ... the masks we wear to cover our true selves

It's little wonder Proverbs 4:23 instructs, "Above all else, guard your heart, for it is the wellspring of life" (NIV). Jesus clearly described how powerful the core beliefs of our hearts become in directing our lives and our legacies.

[20] [Jesus] added, "It is what comes from inside that defiles you. [21] For from within, out of a person's heart, come evil thoughts, sexual immorality, theft, murder, [22] adultery, greed, wickedness, deceit, lustful desires, envy, slander, pride, and foolishness. [23] All these vile things come from within; they are what defile you."

MARK 7:20-23, NLT

LEADER: Discuss as many discovery questions as time permits. It will help to highlight in advance the questions you don't want to miss. Be sensitive to the tender spots of each individual group member.

---

5. According to Jesus in Mark 7:20-23, where do lies, false agreements, and vows become embedded? What impact can these deeply rooted false beliefs have in our lives?

6. Wounds. Lies or false beliefs. Agreements. Vows. Living out of your false self. In which of these areas do you feel the greatest bondage? Please explain.

[8] For you were once darkness [before faith in Jesus], but now you are light in the Lord. Walk as children of light— [9] for the fruit of the light results in all goodness, righteousness, and truth— [10] discerning what is pleasing to the Lord. [11] Don't participate in the fruitless works of darkness, but instead, expose them. ... [13] Everything exposed by the light is made clear. [14] For what makes everything clear is light.

EPHESIANS 5:8-11,13-14A, HCSB

[31] Jesus said ... "If you continue in My word, you really are My disciples. [32] You will know the truth, and the truth will set you free."

JOHN 8:31-32, HCSB

7. The Bible says God is "light" and Jesus is the "Light of the World." According to Ephesians 5:8-11, how do children of light walk?

8. What reasons does God give us for avoiding the darkness and exposing the dark and secret things in our lives (and hearts) to light and truth?

9. What are risks we take in exposing who we really are and the secrets in our lives? What benefits does God promise if we will risk exposure (Ephesians 5:13-14; John 8:32)?

10. Describe what complete freedom would look like to you. According to John 8:31-32, what makes us free, and how do we obtain it?

Embracing the Truth

LEADER: This section's purpose is to help group members integrate what they've learned from the Bible and group discussions into their own hearts and lives. The focus is on accepting the power of sharing our stories within a safe, redemptive group.

The Power of Love

We need to tell our stories to people we trust. This step has a purpose way beyond reopening old wounds—we're here to find recovery, freedom, and healing. God never intended for us to struggle alone. We need each other; we were designed for strong relationships. Amazing things occur when two or more people grasp hands and hearts and share their pain together. God shows up. He does amazing things with people who are humble and open to His supernatural surgery of the heart.

⁹ Two are better than one because they have a good reward for their efforts. ¹⁰ For if either falls, his companion can lift him up; but pity the one who falls without another to lift him up. ¹¹ Also, if two lie down together, they can keep warm; but how can one person alone keep warm? ¹² And if somebody overpowers one person, two can resist him. A cord of three strands is not easily broken.

ECCLESIASTES 4:9-12, HCSB

1. According to Ecclesiastes 4:10-12, in what three situations can we find ourselves when we try to go it alone? In each case, how would it help to have a friend or two with you?

2. Looking at the end of Ecclesiastes 4:12, we see that three people are even better than two in helping us up when we've fallen ethically, spiritually, or physically. In your experience, why is this true? How can you create a "cord of three strands" in your life?

3. Have you ever experienced a deep friendship based on openness and trust? How does it feel when somebody knows who you really are and still wants to be your friend?

It is vital to the healing process to have a group or a person with whom you feel safe—someone who will listen and not judge, who will keep your story confidential, and who will pray with you and for you. You will be encouraged throughout this study to pursue this process with one or more women who will:

• Provide a safe environment where confidences are kept
• Give each other opportunities to share our stories with others who really listen
• Act as "truth mirrors" to help one another see our true selves, not the masks we wear or our insecure, distorted beliefs about other people, God, and ourselves
• Offer acceptance without condemnation (Jesus Himself said to a mob closing in to punish a woman caught in adultery, "Let him who is without sin cast the first stone.").
• Lend each other support, encouragement, and loving accountability.

¹⁶ Make this your common practice: Confess your sins to each other and pray for each other so that you can live together whole and healed. The prayer of a person living right with God is something powerful to be reckoned with. ... ¹⁹ My dear friends, if you know people who have wandered off from God's truth, don't write them off.

Go after them. ²⁰ Get them back and you will have rescued precious lives from destruction and prevented an epidemic of wandering away from God.

JAMES 5:16,19-20, THE MESSAGE

4. What good could come of telling our stories to another person we can trust? How necessary is that? Reread James 5:16,19-20, and then list the advantages of sharing our stories as a group.

As post-abortive women, the thought of being "exposed" or "found out" terrifies us. Most likely, fear of exposure of the pregnancy was a factor in choosing abortion in the first place. That's one reason why many women have guarded their secret for years. But consider this: Whom do we really protect by holding onto the secret? We're covering up the deceiver's lie that abortion doesn't hurt women and we are reinforcing society's belief that we are unaffected by the choice. Remaining silent keeps us in the darkness of the lie, but freedom comes in exposing it.

If you are not part of a healing group, decide today whom you will trust to walk this journey with you. If you are, pray for the other members in your group. They are just as afraid and ashamed as you are. Ask God to help you help one another.

CONNECTING

LEADER: Use "Connecting" as a time to help group members connect with one another, with God, and with their own hearts. See the separate Leader Guide for details and ideas on sharing your story. Invite everyone to share, but do not force people who are not yet ready. Each person's healing journey moves at a different pace.

SHARING OUR STORIES

You will see the amazing power of sharing truth out loud. We're going to spend time breaking the power of secrecy that the enemy has held us under for a long, long time. We're going to share with one another the secret of our darkest hour, secrets tucked away in our darkest places. This will be a giant step in developing trust among our sisters in this group. God will use this time to change your life forever, as you begin to trade a lie for the truth.

Please understand God's desire is not to expose you, leaving you feeling alone and vulnerable. He's a protecting and caring Father who covers His children with grace, not shame. Be courageous; under the protection of God, expose the enemy. Read the following letter from Sheri who, like you, chose to exchange lies for truth. Hear her freedom!

My Dear Sister,

You've made a huge step today! I remember being in your shoes not so long ago and thinking that this was not going to work. Opening up would be impossible for anyone who hurt like I did over my abortion. It was just too personal. The amazing thing I discovered through the process was that I was not alone in my pain and sorrow. All the women in the group shared an ache in their hearts and felt that nobody could understand. Everybody deals with some sort of pain, but we're so fortunate that we've found a group of women who have experienced many of the same things and can help us heal from our hurts.

You can find comfort in this place because you no longer have to pretend to be anything or anyone that you're not. You will cry, laugh, and pray together. I found so much healing from God that I'd always heard about but just couldn't possibly imagine He would extend to me in the mess my life was in. Once I understood that He had forgiven me, over time I was able to forgive myself.

The decision to heal must come from your heart; no one can force you into anything. I found that I had to express and accept my pain before I could move into true healing. Healing won't happen the first time you open up, so don't be discouraged. When I left the first meeting, I felt like I wouldn't come back, but I did. I kept persevering and finished the journey. It was all worth it! Hang in there. Start courageously and finish strong!

Your Sister in Christ, Sheri

As you share the story of your abortion experience with your prayer partner or your healing group, refer to last week's "Taking Truth Home" journal. The questions below may help you get started. You may have held onto this secret so long that it could take a few attempts to remember details. Take your time, ask God to help you, and allow your sisters to hold your hands as you hold theirs.

SHARE YOUR STORY THOUGHT-STARTERS
- What were your life circumstances and relationships like at the time of your abortion?
- Was there anyone in your life you felt you could completely trust?

- When or how did the idea of abortion come to mind? What other options did you consider?
- Describe your abortion experience.
- Share thoughts and feelings you recall before, during, and after the abortion.
- What about you changed the day of the abortion?

What is your greatest need for prayer and practical support right now?

MY PRAYER AND SUPPORT NEEDS

MY GROUP'S PRAYER AND SUPPORT NEEDS

TAKING TRUTH HOME

QUESTIONS TO TAKE TO MY HEART

The following questions ask you to look into your heart and focus on your deepest feelings about yourself and God. Our behaviors are the best indicators of what we really believe deep down. Look deep into the underlying beliefs in your heart where your truest attitudes and motives live. (See Psalm 51:6.) Reflect on the experience of sharing your story with your group.

✳ Thousands of women have walked the healing journey before, women like Sheri whose letter of encouragement we read. How does it feel to know I'm not alone?

✳ How did I feel about opening up and beginning to share my story? What's the worst thing that could happen if I decide to trust God and allow Him to take me back into my pain—my secrets, shadows, and shame?

Questions to Take to God

When you ask God a question, expect His Spirit to respond to your heart. Be careful not to rush it or to manufacture an answer. Don't turn the Bible into a reference book or spiritual encyclopedia. Just pose the question to God, and wait on Him. The litmus test for anything we hear from God is alignment with the Bible as our ultimate truth source.

✳ God, what do You want to say to me about wounds and burdens from my childhood? from my abortion?

✳ Psalm 17:8 pleads, "[God,] Guard me as the apple of Your eye; hide me in the shadow of Your wings." Am I really the apple of Your eye? Do You really cherish me?

RESEARCH AND JOURNAL EXERCISE

The next step on our journey is to face some difficult truths about abortion. In order to heal, we have to make the connection between the abortion experience and our behaviors. When we understand the truth about abortion, we are better able to understand our feelings and behaviors. To prepare for session 3, visit the following Web sites that offer information about the extent of abortion and its devastating effects on our culture and individual lives:

- *www.care-net.org*
- *www.heartbeatinternational.org*
- *www.justthefacts.org*
- *www.awpm.net*
- *www.surrenderingthesecret.com*
- *www.surrenderingthesecret.blogspot.com*

Write a poem, song, letter, or prayer, or draw a picture of how you feel after reviewing the information about abortion on the Web sites. We will share with each other what we've written or created at the next meeting together.

MY FEELINGS ABOUT ABORTION

Pat's Journal Entry 3

I knew before they spoke it,
As women often do,
That a life had formed inside me
Though I prayed it not be true.

In an instant, I was not alone,
Fear stood by constantly.
It attacked my thoughts in dark, black moods,
"How could this have happened to me?"

I do not want this baby
There is no other way; "GET RID OF IT"
Were words I heard.
It seemed a small price to pay.

The whiteness of the ceiling,
Bright lights and sharp cold air
Are vivid in my memories.
I never knew I'd care.

Years went past with only fleeting thoughts of
What might have been.
But never did it dawn on me that
Murder is a sin.

It never seemed to me that way,
Until one awful night,
A nightmare broke into my sleep,
I screamed and cried with fright.

I could see the Lord beside me,
By that table, in that place,
I saw His eyes and heard His voice,
And tears streamed down His face.

In a broken voice He said to me,
"My daughter, tell me why?
I worked with love to make that child
For you to let it die."

Since that meeting with the Lord,
He's healed my wounds and sins,
But I'll never be completely healed
Until ABORTION ENDS.

Pat Layton

WALK IN TRUTH

BREAKING THE ICE

LEADER: *"Breaking the Ice" is designed to help group members settle into the group setting and to put them at ease when talking about today's difficult topic. Remember, the more connected group members are, the more open and healing the group will become. See the separate Leader Guide for additional support ideas. Watch the video for session 3 (optional).*

---

1. What were some of your favorite childhood games? What did you enjoy about them?

2. Which hiding game did you play as a child: Hide and Seek, Sardines, Ghost in the Grave Yard, Kick the Can, or Marco Polo? What was your best strategy for playing?

Have you ever played Hide and Seek with a small child and watched as they "hide" their very visible little bodies behind open chairs or small tables? They think they're completely out of your sight, but they're hiding strategies are completely ineffective with an adult. Being found can be fun, but if no one looked for you or ever found you, Hide and Seek would be a tragedy.

3. Have you ever felt your life was slowly fading away and no one was looking for you? Explain.

4. During this past week, what did you hear from God about His feelings related to your wounds, your abortion, or your personal life?

OPENING PRAYER

Father, in my "Taking Truth Home" assignment, I read that I am "the apple of Your eye"—deeply cherished. When life gets difficult, I often feel like hiding. One of my greatest fears is that nobody will come find me. I want to believe that You care about my pain. I want to believe that You care enough about me to come and find me when I'm lost. Abba, Daddy, help my unbelief. Come find me, even when I'm hiding from You. Walk with me on this journey, and draw me closer and closer to Your heart.

OBJECTIVES FOR THIS SESSION
- Recognize that we live in a world of deception
- Explore the negative affects of abortion on women
- Discuss reasons women choose abortions
- Accept the truth about life, embryos, and God's plans
- Understand how God views our abortions and the dark places into which we slide
- Challenge ourselves to make the choice to heal

DISCOVERING THE TRUTH

LEADER: The goal of "Discovering the Truth" is to expose deceptions and issues related to abortion and to begin to walk in the truth. Encourage all group members to join the discussion. Be sure to keep things moving.

In our last session together we discovered the process of deception the enemy uses to rob you of freedom and life. Sharing your story was a difficult but strong step forward. We'll continue the journey into truth in session 3 as we unravel some big deceptions related to abortion.

MY HEALING JOURNEY

SHARING THE
SECRET: A SPRING
IN THE
DESERT

WALK IN
TRUTH

WHERE HAVE
YOU COME
FROM?

VOICES OF DECEPTION

In session 2, we discussed that lying is innate in children. Unfortunately, lying does not end with childhood. The Devil is the father of lies and continues to pour his twisted deceptions into our world. We've seen God's wonderful heart toward us and our pain. Let's see how He feels about deception.

Lying lips are detestable to the LORD, but faithful people are His delight.

PROVERBS 12:22, HCSB

[16] There are six things the LORD hates, seven that are detestable to him: [17] haughty eyes, a lying tongue, hands that shed innocent blood, [18] a heart that devises wicked schemes, feet that are quick to rush into evil, [19] a false witness who pours out lies and a man who stirs up dissension among brothers.

PROVERBS 6:16-19, NIV

> LEADER: *Discuss as many discovery questions as time permits. The purpose of this section is to show how we all fall for the lies of the enemy. It is not intended to cause guilt.*

1. Why do you think Proverbs says that lying is "detestable" to God? Why might it be among the top things He hates?

2. What damage can lies, deception, and twisted information bring into people's lives? Give an example.

God's purposes in giving us laws is never to make us miserable or to control us but to protect us by setting boundaries and guidelines for our own good. We learned from John 10:32 that "the truth will set you free." No lie ever has or ever will bring freedom.

BROKEN TRUSTS

Whether people lie for their own gain, to protect themselves or because they have themselves bought into the deception, lies hurt. The power of a lie is that if we believe it to be true, we will act on it as truth. God warns us about deception in our world:

[3] *"They make ready their tongue like a bow, to shoot lies; it is not by truth that they triumph in the land. They go from one sin to another; they do not acknowledge me," declares the Lord.* [4] *"Everyone has to be on guard against his friend. Don't trust any brother, for every brother will certainly deceive, and every friend spread slander.* [5] *Each one betrays his friend; no one tells the truth. They have taught their tongues to speak lies; they wear themselves out doing wrong.* [6] *You live in a world of deception. In their deception they refuse to know Me. This is the Lord's declaration."*

JEREMIAH 9:4-6, HCSB

3. According to verses 3 and 6, why do we live in a world of deception? Discuss places in our culture where deception prevails and trust has eroded.

4. As you look back on your abortion experience, what lies or shaded truths do you hear? In hindsight, how do you know that you did not have the whole truth?

BE AWARE!

1) We have an enemy. (1 Peter 5:8)

2) His greatest tool is deception. (2 Corinthians 11:3)

3) His favorite tactic is causing us to question God's instructions. (Genesis 3:1)

4) He always challenges God's character and goodness. (Genesis 3:4)

5) His ultimate goal is broken relationships with God and others. (Genesis 3:6)

THE SIDE OF ABORTION NOBODY EVER TELLS YOU

For many women, their first emotion after having an abortion is immediate relief—relief that they're no longer burdened with an unplanned, unwanted pregnancy. Research indicates, however, that this relief is short-lived and is soon replaced by guilt, shame, secrecy, sadness, and regret. This strong letdown experience is commonly referred to as Post-Abortion Trauma. Approximately 40 percent of post-abortive women experience intense traumatic responses to abortion; however, statistics reveal that 80 percent will experience some level of symptoms. Some psychologists believe the statistic is actually as high as 100 percent of women who suffer some measure of trauma.

REVIEW THESE ALARMING STATISTICS ON THE NEGATIVE AFFECTS OF ABORTION[1]

- 92% of women who've had abortions experience emotional deadening
- 86% experience anger or rage
- 86% fear others finding out
- 82% experience intense feelings of loneliness or isolation
- 63% experience denial
- 58% battle nightmares
- 56% develop suicidal feelings
- 53% engage in drug abuse
- 39% have eating disorders

We are everywhere ... women who have bought the enemy's lie that abortion was our only hope, our only choice, and what we "had to do." The Alan Guttmacher Institute, a division of Planned Parenthood, estimates that 43 percent of American women will have an abortion by age 45. The institute also suggests that half of all pregnancies in the U.S. are unintended; out of those, 4 in 10 will end in abortion. In the U.S. alone, more than 1.5 million abortions are performed each year, making abortion one of the most common surgical procedures performed on women today. [2]

5. Do any of these statistics surprise you? How does this information make you feel about abortion?

WHY WOMEN GET ABORTIONS[3]

- 75% said their baby would interfere with their lives
- 66% said they couldn't afford a child
- 50% didn't want to be a mother at the time
- 4% had a doctor who said their health would worsen with the baby
- 1% had a fetal abnormality
- 1% were victims of rape or incest

6. What part did your relationship with your child's father play in your decision? Was he involved? Did he know about your choice?

7. Do you feel that you had all of the truth when you made your abortion decision? Explain. How have your feelings changed since you first had an abortion?

ACCEPTING THE TRUTH ABOUT LIFE

Heated debate about when life begins still exists, but the Creator of life gives us a perspective we can't ignore about the lives of mothers and babies.

[13] Oh yes, you shaped me first inside, then out; you formed me in my mother's womb. [14] I thank you, High God—you're breathtaking! Body and soul, I am marvelously made! I worship in adoration—what a creation! [15] You know me inside and out, you know every bone in my body; You know exactly how I was made, bit by bit, how I was sculpted from nothing into something. [16] Like an open book, you watched me grow from conception to birth; all the stages of my life were spread out before you, the days of my life all prepared before I'd even lived one day.

PSALM 139:13-16, THE MESSAGE

8. According to Psalm 139, who's the Giver and Creator of life? What does this psalm highlight about how a life is created (verses 13,15)? about when life begins (verses 13,16)?

9. What does verse 16 say about God's plan for life? What about those children we think are mistakes?

LEADER: Share good color photos, illustrations, or videos that demonstrate a baby's development at various stages of pregnancy with your group now. In advance, download the free video called Baby 4-D Sonogram from www.SerendipityHouse.com/Downloads.aspx. The video will play directly on a computer, on any display screen that connects to your computer, or on some newer DVD systems that play Windows Media WMV files. However, to play this on most DVD systems requires that you convert this file using DVD authoring software. If you do not have a DVD authoring program on your computer, you may purchase one at a software retailer or online.

See the separate Leader Guide for ideas for powerful listening prayer time instructions.

4-D Sonogram

As you watch the video of a baby in utero, you will marvel and you will also remember and grieve your loss. Remember, you are with friends who care deeply about you.

We don't understand the amazing elements of creating a person's soul, but the physical development alone is beyond what most of us would imagine:

- At 7 days the new life has developed its own blood cells; the placenta is a part of the new life and not of the mother.
- At 19 days the heart begins to beat.
- At 20 days the foundation of the entire nervous system has been laid down.
- At 24 days the heart has regular beats or pulsations.
- At 30 days there is regular blood flow within the vascular system; ear and nasal development have begun.
- At 35 days eyes start to develop and 40 pairs of muscles are present.
- At 40 days the heart energy output is reported to be almost 20 percent of an adult level.
- At 42 days brain waves are detectable. This is usually ample evidence that "thinking" is taking place in the brain. The new life may be thought of as a thinking person.
- At 49 days the skeletal system is developed. The baby appears as a miniature doll with complete fingers, toes, and ears.
- At 50 days all internal organs and external structures are identifiable.
- At 56 days all organs are functioning—stomach, liver, kidney, brain—all systems intact. All future development of new life is simply growth and maturity of what is there.
- At the 9th and 10th weeks the teeth begin to form, fingernails develop, and the baby squints, swallows, retracts tongue.
- At the 11th and 12th weeks the baby can grasp objects placed in the hand, hiccups, urinates, and recoils from pain.
- At 13 weeks the baby's sex is identifiable.
- At weeks 16–20 the baby hears external voices, sleeps, and dreams.
- At 21 weeks a child can survive birth.[4]

10. Now that you've read Psalm 139 and discussed the rapid formation of the baby in the womb, what are your thoughts and feelings about abortion? Take a minute or two to write out what's going through your mind, and then share with the group.

11. In what ways do you think your abortion decision affected God's plan for your life? What about God's plan for your unborn child's life?

God knows what your unborn baby was like in every cell of his or her body. He knows what the child would have looked like at 12 years old or as a young adult. Life does not begin with the first breath or the first heartbeat. It begins in the heart and mind of God before conception. Women have been endowed with the incredible ability and opportunity to give life to eternal souls created in the image of God!

EMBRACING THE TRUTH

LEADER: This section helps group members integrate what they've learned from the Bible study and medical discussions into their own hearts and lives. Continue reviewing other parts of Psalm 139 to focus on God's care for the mother's life as well as the baby's.

As we acknowledge the choice to end our baby's life, we tend to retreat back into those dark places in our souls where we feel trapped. But rest peacefully, sweet sister. Jesus knows where you are and He won't abandon you!

Let's read some other parts of Psalm 139:
¹O Lord, you have searched me and you know me. ² You know when I sit and when I rise; you perceive my thoughts from afar. ³ You discern my going out and my lying down; you are familiar with all my ways. ⁴ Before a word is on my tongue you know it completely, O Lord. ⁵ You hem me in—behind and before; you have laid your hand upon me. ⁶ Such knowledge is too wonderful for me, too lofty for me to attain. ⁷ Where can I go from your Spirit? Where can I flee from your presence? ⁸ If I go up to the heavens, you are there; if I make my bed in the depths, you are there. ⁹ If I rise on the wings of the dawn, if I settle on the far side of the sea, ¹⁰ even there your hand will guide me, your right hand will hold me fast. ¹¹ If I say, "Surely the darkness will hide me and the light become night around me," ¹² even the darkness will not be dark to you; the night will shine like the day, for darkness is as light to you.

PSALM 139:1-12, NIV

1. How does it feel to realize that nothing is hidden from God's sight and that He is with you even into the darkest, loneliest, and most difficult parts of your life?

2. Verse 12 says to God, "for darkness is as light to you." In your situation, as you realize that God sees with perfect clarity in the darkness of our souls and deepest secrets, what could it mean for you as you move forward?

3. Do you recall a time in your life when you knew that God was with you? Briefly share your experience with the group, and tell how you felt God's presence. How do you sense God's presence in your life now?

4. Read the following list of emotions and behaviors. Check all of those that apply to you:

❏ Guilt
❏ Shame
❏ Depression
❏ Anxiety
❏ Unworthiness
❏ Fear
❏ Numbness of feelings
❏ Deep regret
❏ Thoughts of suicide
❏ Reduced motivation
❏ Lack of trust

❏ Drug abuse
❏ Alcohol abuse
❏ Abusive relationships
❏ Promiscuity
❏ Acting out in anger and rage
❏ Loss of interest in relationships
❏ Difficulty with intimacy
❏ Difficulty sleeping
❏ Appetite disturbances
❏ Excessive crying
❏ Nightmares

5. Now, circle those feelings or behaviors you *think* may be linked to your abortion. Add any emotions or behaviors you may have felt as a result of your abortion but are not on the list. Share your responses with your prayer partner or group.

6. Do particular situations or circumstances tend to evoke these feelings and behaviors in your life? Why do you think certain situations can act as triggers for harmful reactions?

[3] When I kept silent about my sin, my body wasted away through my groaning all day long. [4] For day and night your hand was heavy upon me, my vitality was drained away as with the fever heat of summer. [5] I acknowledged my sin to you and my iniquity I did not hide. I said, "I will confess my transgressions to the Lord; and you forgave the guilt of my sin."

PSALM 32:3-5, NASB

7. According to Psalm 32, what results from stuffing our feelings and wounds inside rather than turning to God for forgiveness, healing, and freedom?

CONNECTING

> LEADER: Use "Connecting" as a time to help group members connect with each other, with God, and with their own hearts.

OUR RESCUER

Several times we've looked at God's promises of truth, hope, and redemption. Many remedies we have grasped to relieve the pain of our abortions have been offered in dark places. Many of these remedies—including drugs, alcohol, and meaningless relationships with men—are self-destructive. Many of us are going through this healing journey because we've already discovered that we can't find our way out of our dark places alone. Our rescue begins when we acknowledge that we are powerless to heal our lives on our own. Only the Savior can rescue, re-create, and restore us from the inside out.

We've discussed that if we want to experience healing, we must be willing to trust Jesus to take us on the unfamiliar and risky path to it.

Take some time for prayer and reflection, asking God to help you get a deeper insight into all you have considered so far in session 3. It has probably been a lot of new information. You may never have envisioned the child of your abortion as "being knit together by God." Give God time to show you His heart for you as you proceed toward His full healing.

1. How have the enemy's lies pushed me down?

2. How have I been managing the lie—playing along with the enemy's lies—around my family and friends, when I hear about abortion from the church pulpit, when I hear pro-life and pro-choice discussions in the media, and other areas of my life?

God created us in His image (Genesis 1:27) with the freedom of choice. Ever since Adam and Eve chose to disobey God, the world has been anything but paradise. Our freedom to choose has destroyed life across the ages, but God willingly created us with the freedom to make our own decisions. We always have free choice, but choices always have consequences. Before entering the promised land Moses challenged the Israelites saying, "Today I have given you the choice between life and death, between blessings and curses. Now I call on heaven and earth to witness the choice you make. Oh, that you would choose life, so that you and your descendants might live" (Deuteronomy 30:19, NLT).

3. Will you reject the past with its shame, curses, and death, choosing instead the path to life, freedom, and blessing with Jesus? If so, acknowledge to the others in your group that YOU CHOOSE LIFE!

4. Take some time to share the poems, songs, or letters that you wrote at home this week. If you are going through *Surrendering the Secret* by yourself, please share yours with your prayer partner.

How can we pray for you today as you continue to take the path that leads to life and freedom? As you continue to accept the truth about your abortion, with what emotional issues are you struggling? How can we help through prayer or practical support?

My Prayer and Support Needs

My Group's Prayer and Support Needs

Taking Truth Home

You have taken in a lot of new information during this session. Hopefully you have seen yourself and your sisters in the truths we have learned about abortion, what it really does to women, and the huge loss we all experience without the lives of our children. Take some time to reflect on what you feel about what we've discussed.

A Question to Take to My Heart

The following questions ask you to look into your heart and consider with brutal honesty your deepest feelings and beliefs. Remember, our behaviors are the best indicators of what we really believe in our innermost being (Psalm 51:6). Be sure to capture your insights and feelings.

✳ How do I feel about myself and my choice to have an abortion? What lies do I still hold onto that prevent me from feeling the full impact of my decision to end my child's life?

QUESTIONS TO TAKE TO GOD

When you ask God a question, expect His Spirit to respond to your heart. Be careful not to rush it or manufacture an answer. Don't turn the Bible into a reference book or spiritual encyclopedia. Just pose the question to God, and wait on Him. The litmus test for anything we hear from God is alignment with the Bible as our ultimate truth source.

✳ Your Word says that you can see me, Lord. Why do You allow something like abortion to be available to us when You know how much it will hurt? Why didn't you stop me? Where were You?

LETTERS TO PEOPLE INVOLVED IN MY ABORTION

Your pain and many problems in your life are rooted in the fact that abortion stole your unborn child. In your heart and mind, abortion has no doubt left you feeling separated from God and from others. Over the next few sessions we're going to consider all the other people in your life who may have been deceived by the lies of abortion. Some of them may have pressured you to abort, or perhaps they just allowed it to happen without pointing you to another answer.

Based on the things you've learned over the last few weeks about truth and deception, take time to write a letter to each person who was a part of your abortion decision (doctors, boyfriend/husband, church or religious leaders, employer, school counselor, friends, parents, lawmakers, the media, and so forth). Consider how the person was involved and also how he or she might have been affected. Allow yourself to feel sadness, anger, hurt, betrayal, or whatever other feelings you've stuffed deep inside. Open up and express your feelings openly and honestly.

DO NOT MAIL OR DELIVER THESE LETTERS! The purpose for this exercise is for your healing, not to hurt someone else. Bring them to the meeting for session 4 or share them with a trusted prayer partner or leader. You'll understand more about this process as we move along.

NOTES

1. and 3. Medical and statistical information was taken from the article, "Medical Report/Women's Health/Abortion ... Is There a Connection?" NOEL: noelinfo@noelforlife.org, accessed October 25, 2006.
2. "Abortion Data from Reports of the Alan Guttmacher Institute": www.religioustolerance.org/abo_fact3.htm, accessed November 15, 2006.
4. Vera L. Bailey. "Fetal Development," Students for Life of America [online] 28 June 2001 [cited 2 April 2007]. Available from the Internet: http://www.studentsforlife.org/wp/education/fetal-development/

Just hours ago I had struggled to open my eyes. Now, as my parents stood numbly at the foot of my hospital bed, I was struggling to close them.

"They" said that the whole procedure would be over in 30 minutes. "They" said I would be picking up my five-year-old son from school that afternoon. "They" said a few aspirin would do the trick after the procedure. Nothing "they" said was true.

My abortion was supposed to be a three-hour break in my busy day, allowing me to be on my way by noon. Instead, I had an allergic reaction to the anesthesia they used to put me to sleep, and "they" had to put me on a respirator to keep me alive. By noon I was still unable to breath on my own, much less pick up my son from school. I had to call on my parents to do that for me. Of course, after they picked up my boy, my parents rushed to the hospital. And "they" had said no one would even have to know. Nothing "they" said was true.

"They" said there was "no need to worry" about the fever and the cramps that lasted five days after I went home from the hospital. As I grew worse, "they" changed their minds and said, "We are very sorry" and admitted me back into the hospital. "They" said, "During the emergency we encountered during your first procedure, parts of the fetus were left behind. We will need to repeat the procedure."

I never even thought about the word "fetus" as "they" said it. All I could think was "baby." My baby. "Parts" left behind? Which "parts"? The heart? The hands? The parts of a boy or a girl? My God, which parts? Nothing "they" said was true.

A TIME FOR ANGER
TEARING DOWN ROADBLOCKS

BREAKING THE ICE

LEADER: See the separate Leader Guide for detailed instructions for the group experience. Show the video for session 4 (optional).

Using the materials supplied by your leader, create a collage that represents the "mask" that you've worn—the face that you've presented to other people with whom you can't share your secret. Cut out or draw images that illustrate how you've coped with your emotions during your years of silence. You'll have about 10 minutes to finish it before each person presents and explains her "mask" to the group. Don't aim for perfection; focus on identifying your coping mechanisms. Show your mask to your group and briefly describe the reasoning behind your creation. Identify your primary coping mechanisms.

1. What messages about expressing anger were you given in your home as you were growing up? How did adults in your home express anger?

2. As you reflected back this week on the death of your child, what emotions did you experience?

OPENING PRAYER

Lord, I confess that at times my anger can control me, and sometimes I try to stuff it down inside my heart rather than effectively dealing with it. Having anger is like receiving a package of mysterious parts without instructions. It's mine, but I don't really know what it is, how to cope with it, or how to use it. I have some of my own ways of dealing with anger, but they really aren't working well for me. Help me, Holy Spirit, to understand this familiar but unwelcome emotion. Teach me healthier ways to express anger and learn from it.

OBJECTIVES FOR THIS SESSION

- Understand that I have the right to be angry
- Discover the underlying roots of anger
- Identify anger in my life that is connected to my abortion(s)
- Recognize unhealthy and ungodly expressions of anger
- Learn healthy ways to direct and express anger toward those involved in the abortion decision

DISCOVERING THE TRUTH

LEADER: *In "Discovering the Truth" the group will begin to unravel some of the tangled roots of anger. The dangers of anger will be discussed. The group will also learn that anger is a powerful emotion that can be used constructively.*

Last week you made a breakthrough in your healing journey by acknowledging the truth about your unborn child and God's plan for life. You've been courageous enough to allow the walls of denial to come down; you've faced the truth about abortion's role in your own life and in the world. You have accomplished so much! As we begin to process the truth about our abortions, anger is one of the key emotions that will and should surface.

MY HEALING JOURNEY

Sharing the
Secret: A Spring
in the
Desert

A Time for Anger:
Tearing Down
Roadblocks

Walk in
Truth

Where Have
You Come
From?

Taking Off the Masks

God created our emotions—including anger—for our benefit. But when we don't use emotions properly, we can do a lot of damage to ourselves and to others. The Bible has plenty to say about how to handle our emotions the right way. Let's look at a verse in Ephesians that shows that anger isn't necessarily a sin.

²⁵ Laying aside falsehood, speak the truth each of you with his neighbor, for we are all members of one another.
²⁶ Be angry, and yet do not sin.

Ephesians 4:25-26, NASB

1. The Greek word for "falsehood" literally refers to the masks that were used in Greek theatre. What does this verse say about our need to be real with each other?

2. Why do we try to hide our hurt or pain? Why is it sometimes difficult to be honest about our feelings? What do you think would happen if we risked being real with God, ourselves, and our friends instead of hiding behind our masks?

3. According to Ephesians 4:25 is anger OK? What are some of the ways we express anger that may cause us to sin against God or hurt other people?

A Right to Be Angry

"Be angry" in Ephesians 4:25 is in the Greek imperative tense used for commands or direct instructions. In this passage God actually commands us to be angry! Let's look at two anger stories in the Bible. The first is that of the young Moses, an Israelite slave in Egypt whom God had miraculously spared from slaughter through his mother's clever plan. Moses was actually raised into a position of great influence in the house of Pharaoh's daughter, but the events of one day changed all that.

[11] Years later, after Moses had grown up, he went out to his own people and observed their forced labor. He saw an Egyptian beating a Hebrew, one of his people. [12] Looking all around and seeing no one, he struck the Egyptian dead and hid him in the sand. [13] The next day he went out and saw two Hebrews fighting. He asked the one in the wrong, "Why are you attacking your neighbor?" [14] "Who made you a leader and judge over us?" the man replied. "Are you planning to kill me as you killed the Egyptian?" Then Moses became afraid and thought: What I did is certainly known. [15] When Pharaoh heard about this, he tried to kill Moses. But Moses fled from Pharaoh and went to live in the land of Midian.

Exodus 2:11-15, HCSB

4. What stirred Moses' anger and how did he respond to it (verses 11-12)? Was his anger justified? Explain.

5. Was Moses' response to his anger healthy and constructive in solving Israel's problems? List constructive ways Moses could have channeled his anger.

When Jesus saw how temple businessmen were cheating and extorting people who came to the temple to worship God, He too demonstrated anger:

¹⁰ *The entire city of Jerusalem was in an uproar as he entered. "Who is this?" they asked. ¹¹ And the crowds replied, "It's Jesus, the prophet from Nazareth in Galilee." ¹² Jesus entered the Temple and began to drive out all the people buying and selling animals for sacrifice. He knocked over the tables of the money changers and the chairs of those selling doves. ¹³ He said to them, "The Scriptures declare, 'My Temple will be called a house of prayer,' but you have turned it into a den of thieves!"*

MATTHEW 21:10-13, NLT

6. In what ways did Jesus' response to anger differ from that of Moses? Would you characterize Jesus' anger as more healthy and constructive? Explain.

7. Why would God encourage us to feel and express anger? When is anger justified rather than just being a means to selfish gain or a way to hurt someone?

Anger is almost always rooted in other emotions such as fear, betrayal, injustice, and selfish ambition. Two key root emotions are (1) hurt or betrayal, and (2) frustration due to blockage of our goals. For example, we may feel our character was questioned or attacked, our rights were violated, our authority defied, or something or someone we value was dishonored. These are only a couple of examples, but you get the idea—an underlying thought or feeling works its way through the assembly line of our mental factory and comes out as anger. Anger is a God-given emotion that helps us address issues, but it must be handled carefully. The goal must always be helping others, our relationships, and ourselves in the long run.

IMPLODERS AND EXPLODERS

Two unhealthy ways of managing anger are (1) expressing it aggressively, or (2) stuffing it. Dr. Gary Chapman calls these methods explosive and implosive ways of handling anger. Implosive anger is internalized anger that's never expressed. "I'm not angry, just frustrated" or "I'm not mad, just disappointed" are common expressions of an imploder.

²⁵ Therefore, laying aside falsehood, speak the truth each one of you with his neighbor, for we are members of one another. ²⁶ Be angry, and yet do not sin; do not let the sun go down on your anger, ²⁷ and do not give the devil an opportunity. ²⁸ He who steals must steal no longer; but rather he must labor, performing with his own hands what is good, so that he will have something to share with one who has need. ²⁹ Let no unwholesome word proceed from your mouth, but only such a word as is good for edification according to the need of the moment, so that it will give grace to those who hear. ³⁰ Do not grieve the Holy Spirit of God, by whom you were sealed for the day of redemption. ³¹ Let all bitterness and wrath and anger and clamor and slander be put away from you, along with all malice. ³² Be kind to one another, tender-hearted, forgiving each other, just as God in Christ also has forgiven you.

EPHESIANS 4:25-32, NASB

8. What are the results of unexpressed or bottled up anger (Ephesians 4:27-32)?

9. In Ephesians 4:29, the word for "unwholesome" means "rotten." How does anger turn to rottenness? According to Ephesians 4:29-30, what does stuffed anger eventually become?

The results of implosive anger are passive-aggressive behavior, displaced anger, physiological and emotional stress, resentment, bitterness, and hatred. Imploders typically keep score, so the potential for a delayed explosion from a dormant volcano is always there.

When Paul advised, "Do not let the sun go down on your anger," he was telling us to deal with anger promptly and effectively before it spreads and does more damage. He also warned, "Do not give the devil an opportunity." Paul explained that poorly managed anger offers the Devil a "*topos*"—a plot of land in our lives. He uses that *topos* as a military base from which to launch more attacks into our lives and relationships.

Explosive anger is the other unhealthy, ungodly management technique. It's characterized by uncontrolled fury that may manifest in verbal and/or physical abuse.

10. What is typically the outcome of all poorly managed anger (Ephesians 4:31)?

11. How would you define explosive anger? Describe a time you've experienced explosive words or behavior and how it made you feel.

Explosive anger verbally attacks by screaming, cursing, condemning, name-calling, humiliating, or threatening. It damages self-esteem and trust and ultimately destroys a relationship when the exploder causes the anger recipient to retreat for emotional safety. Exploders frequently blame their victims for their anger or minimize their outbursts by calling them "blowing off steam" or "getting something off my chest." In extreme cases, the exploder may grab, push, or strike in anger. All unhealthy anger is harmful, but physical abuse is intolerable and protective measures should be sought. Don't try to justify or rationalize explosive anger—get rid of it and replace it with healthy approaches!

EMBRACING THE TRUTH

UNRAVELING OUR ANGER

Don't sin by letting anger control you. Think about it overnight and remain silent.

PSALM 4:4, NLT

Look after each other so that none of you fails to receive the grace of God. Watch out that no poisonous root of bitterness grows up to trouble you, corrupting many.

HEBREWS 12:15, NLT

1. Psalm 4:4 says that we sin when we let our anger gain control. How can anger gain control over you? What are some of the signs that it has?

2. It's been said that anger is contagious. Do you agree? Explain. According to Hebrews 12:15, what can happen if we leave anger unresolved?

Unresolved anger finds unhealthy ways to express itself. Gary Chapman, author of *The Five Languages of Apology* says, "When one's sense of right is violated, that person will experience anger. He or she will feel wronged and resentful at the person (or persons) who have violated their trust. The wrongful act stands as a barrier between the two people and the relationship is fractured. They cannot, even if they desired, live as though the wrong had not been committed. Something inside the offended calls for justice." At the same time, he also acknowledges, "Something inside cries out for reconciliation."[1]

Post-abortive women often react to things in ways they don't understand. They find themselves overreacting to events and circumstances in ways they don't expect—sometimes with anger, or other times with great sadness or hurt. Now that you are on your healing journey, you can begin to make sense of these uncomfortable emotions.

3. Review this list of situations and circumstances that might trigger your anger. Check all that apply to you. Think about events and situations that have been uncomfortable for you, perhaps as a result of your abortion decisions. Anger triggers include:

❒ Baby showers
❒ Mothers with children
❒ Books about fetal development
❒ Doctor visits
❒ Certain smells and odors
❒ Literature related to abortion
❒ Other:_____

❒ Pregnant women
❒ Hospital nurseries and birth events
❒ Videos and TV programs related to pregnancy and birth
❒ Specific sounds
❒ Pro-life/Pro-choice advertisements and commercials

4. Women describe many different responses to these triggers. How do you typically cope with abortion-related anger or situations that stir up bad feelings that you cannot connect to a specific cause?

As we come face-to-face with our abortion decision, we're reminded of people who were involved in that choice. As we reflect on these people and their influence, we're reminded of the confusion, pressure, and perhaps the feeling that we had no other choice. As a result, a woman may aim her post-abortion anger at many targets.

5. Review this list of potential anger targets. Check all that apply to you. While you may not feel angry with a particular person, check anyone whom you hold even partly responsible for your pregnancy or abortion decision. Anger targets include:

❒ Those who withheld the truth about abortion
❒ Friends who presented abortions as the best choice
❒ Yourself for allowing the unplanned pregnancy
❒ Doctors and nurses
❒ Extended family members
❒ Teachers or school counselors
❒ Church and religious leaders
Other: _____

❒ The father of the baby
❒ Parents
❒ God
❒ The abortion clinic
❒ The baby
❒ Media
❒ Lawmakers

Often we hesitate to admit our anger toward others for fear of rejection. We find ourselves defending those we feel we should love. In order to heal, it's important to acknowledge anger and release it in a healthy way.

CONNECTING

LEADER: *Ephesians 4:25-32 provides an effective anger checklist to help manage this God-given emotion in a godly way.*

EPHESIANS ANGER CHECKLIST

❒ ASSESS YOUR PRIMARY EMOTION: Does my anger stem from loss of control, hurt, or indignation about wrongs?
❒ TAKE OFF YOUR MASK: Open up about what hurt you and talk through your feelings (Ephesians 4:25-26).
❒ DEAL WITH ISSUES AND CONFRONT: Communicate issues clearly and early. Be sure the goal is resolving issues, not getting back at people (Ephesians 4:28). When confrontation is not feasible, writing an "angry letter" *you don't send* is very healing.
❒ DON'T LET ANGER FESTER AND ROT: Unresolved anger is a written invitation to the enemy to exploit us in wounding ourselves and others (Ephesians 4:29).
❒ GOD CARES DEEPLY ABOUT YOUR ANGER: Turn your anger over to God. His heart aches when we allow rage, resentment, or bitterness to root (Ephesians 4:30).
❒ REPLACE ANGER WITH FORGIVENESS AND COMPASSION: Because God has forgiven us so much, we need to be willing to forgive others (Ephesians 4:32).

ANGRY LETTERS

Your "Taking Truth Home" assignment in session 3 involved writing letters to some of the people involved in your abortion decision. You may even need to write an angry letter to God. Don't be afraid of this. God is big enough to handle your emotions and will help you work through them. He longs for you to pour out your heart to Him. Remember, you don't have to write a letter for *every* angry target. Allow God to show you which people or situations need to be faced and which need to be overlooked. DO NOT MAIL or show the letters to the "Targets." God wants to use this exercise to heal you, not hurt others. He will handle their hearts His way!

1. It's time to share your angry letter(s) with your group or prayer partner. Simply read your letter out loud. Sometimes it is better to allow someone in your healing group or your prayer partner to read the letter back to you.

LEADER: *Refer to session 4 in the separate Leader Guide for additional ideas on how to complete the exercise.*

2. Once everyone in your group has shared her letter, wad your letter into a tight ball. Then unfold it, rip it to shreds, and discard it in a trash can. Did you get rid of your anger by wadding up your letter, shredding it, and discarding it in the trash? Why or why not?

The truth is that the issues that made us angry are still with us even though we shred the letters. Your healing journey is a process. Even if you've somehow been able to eliminate all your anger to date, another issue will soon require reassessing your anger management. Ongoing communication, negotiation, decision-making, and conflict resolution are realities and necessities of a life made up of relationships. The good news is that anger doesn't have to consume or control you. You can learn to appropriately respond to anger and can choose to express it in healthy ways that make things better.

3. How can we pray for you today as you allow yourself to feel your buried emotions and take them to God to receive healing and the power to forgive? How can we help through prayer or practical support this week?

My Prayer and Support Needs

My Group's Prayer and Support Needs

LEADER: *Emphasize that dealing with anger and forgiveness is a process that takes time. Encourage them to be patient but continue to take steps forward.*

Taking Truth Home

Questions to Take to My Heart

Look into your heart for the answers to these questions. This is introspection time—time to grapple with what drives your thinking and behavior. Every action has a corresponding belief that drives it. Dig for what you believe in the deepest recesses of your heart about God, yourself, and the world in which you live. Be sure to journal your thoughts.

✲ How do I express my anger in ungodly or unhealthy ways? What's really behind my anger and responses? What repeated messages do I hear playing in my mind about God, myself, or the people involved in my abortion?

Questions to Take to God

When you ask God a question, expect His Spirit to respond to your heart. Be careful not to rush it or manufacture an answer. Don't turn the Bible into a reference book or spiritual encyclopedia. Just pose the question to God, and wait on Him. The litmus test for anything we hear from God is alignment with the Bible as our ultimate truth source.

✳ God, I have numbed my feelings for so long that sometimes I don't really feel any anger toward others about my abortion, even when I should. God, how do You feel about abortion and what it's done to women and Your creation?

✳ God, are You angry with me? It's not easy to admit my anger at You. What do You think of my anger toward You? What do You want to say to me about my abortion?

Journal Exercise

Once we have faced our anger, the next challenge is the journey to forgiveness. There are three areas of forgiveness: forgiving others, forgiving ourselves, and accepting God's forgiveness. This will be the focus of session 5. Forgiveness is a process that starts with willingness and ends with taking people off the hook for punishment.

This week's journal activity involves writing two additional letters. First, write a letter to yourself that expresses any leftover thoughts or feelings of anger or disappointment related to your abortion decision.

Then, write another letter as if it were from God to another woman who has experienced an abortion and is searching for healing. Sometimes it helps to picture the faces of women in your group or someone you know and love who may have faced an abortion decision. What do you think God would want to tell them at this point of the journey?

NOTE
1. Gary Chapman, *The Five Languages of Apology* (Northfield Publishing, 2006)

LETTERS FROM ME AND FROM HEAVEN

PAT'S JOURNAL ENTRY 5

It was a fabulous Florida day. Springtime. My windows were rolled down and my Christian music was blaring. I was singing and praising God because I'd recently experienced a dramatic spiritual rebirth. My husband and two sons had also turned to Christ. God was pouring out His blessings on our home and family, but my secret was still happily tucked away.

I left my car for a few minutes to run an errand. When I slid back into the driver's seat, my praise music had changed over to a talk show. I was shocked to hear three women talking with a moderator, sharing their stories about past abortions.

I could barely breathe as I listened. My heart raced. What in the world was this? Abortion! Why were they talking about that on a Christian radio station? What does God have to do with abortion? What does abortion have to do with God? What had happened to my praise music?

Little did I know as I pulled my car to the side of the road to listen that my life would never be the same again.

A few months later, after I'd successfully stuffed my emotions down again, I strolled into the Christian bookstore with one thing in mind: to fix my husband! He really needed fixing. We had been Christians for at least a year and I just knew God still wanted to do a lot of work on him. As I stepped into the bookstore, I ran smack into a display of books all focused on one topic—you guessed it—abortion. Here it was again—right in my face. The book that caught my eye was **Will I Cry Tomorrow?** I grabbed it up, dashed to the register, paid the bill, and raced for the door.

Over the next five or six hours, I devoured the book from cover to cover. After finishing, I fumbled my way to the bathtub and filled it halfway with very hot water. The rest of the tub I filled with my tears as I sobbed for hours. I wept for my aborted child. I wept for my loss. I wept for the lies. I wept for the author of the book I'd read. I wept for the abortionists involved in our lives. I wept for the world. I wept for the pain of my Savior, my Lord, and my Redeemer, Jesus Christ.

When I had cried all that I could cry, I handed my heart to God.

SESSION 5

FORGIVENESS
A GIANT STEP TOWARD FREEDOM

BREAKING THE ICE

LEADER: Dealing with emotions can be draining. Many group members may have experienced a tough week of wrestling with feelings. Allow time for participants to share how their week has been. Watch the video for session 5 (optional).

You have made such progress. Even starting this difficult journey was a major accomplishment, but you may not feel wonderful as you begin this week. You have looked at truth, you have taken some time to face your anger—the good, bad and ugly of it.

1. Discuss with one another about how you are feeling at this stage of your journey. (If you're working through this on your own, talk to God about how you're doing.) Here's a phrase to help you get started: "One of the hardest things about letting go of my anger is ..."

The process of working through anger can be exhausting, but releasing anger lightens the load on your healing journey. This week the goal is to work through anger, to continue to let go, and to start moving toward forgiveness.

2. As you spent time alone and in listening to God this week, what insights did you gain into your feelings surrounding your abortion?

Opening Prayer

Jesus, You paid the price for my forgiveness by Your sacrifice on the cross. Forgiveness always requires a sacrifice on the part of the one who forgives, and I'm not sure I'm up to the challenge. I know I'll need Your supernatural power and courage. Meet me here, and help me gain a clear view of forgiveness. Help me to forgive others as You have forgiven me.

Objectives for this Session

- Increase openness to the concept of forgiveness
- Recognize what true forgiveness is and is not
- Understand the benefits of forgiveness and the consequences of not forgiving
- Separate the conscious choice of forgiving from our emotions
- Verbalize an understanding of God's forgiveness in our own lives

As you begin to let go of your anger, think of it as healing you. Put the burden of resentment in God's hands. Holding on to anger and unforgiveness is like drinking poison and waiting for someone else to die from its effects. Last week, we symbolically released our anger towards the people involved in our abortion experience by destroying the letters we had written them. In this session we will look at the healing that comes from not just letting anger go but actually forgiving those who hurt us. It will set us free!

Discovering the Truth

LEADER: *In the initial part of "Discovering the Truth," you will begin to share with the group what forgiveness is not. Discussions will then examine true, healing forgiveness.*

Last week we looked at the people involved in your abortion. You may find yourself saying, "I want to stop being angry, but I just can't." If we want to experience true healing, we have to at some point make a decision to let go of our anger. The truth is, God wants us to go a step further: He wants us to forgive! In an area of our lives where we have been so hurt, it's difficult to imagine forgiving some of our offenders. But we can do it!

MY HEALING JOURNEY

SHARING THE SECRET: A SPRING IN THE DESERT

WALK IN TRUTH

A TIME FOR ANGER: TEARING DOWN ROADBLOCKS

WHERE HAVE YOU COME FROM?

FORGIVENESS: A GIANT STEP TOWARD FREEDOM

1. How would you explain or describe forgiveness?

In referring to His people, God says:
I will forgive their wickedness and will remember their sins no more.

JEREMIAH 31:34B, NIV

2. According to Jeremiah, how does God forgive?

FORGIVENESS ISN'T ...
Before we define what genuine forgiveness is and make a case for its necessity in healing, let's first clarify what forgiveness is not.

Forgiveness is NOT forgetting.
We frequently hear the phrase "forgive and forget," but forgiveness does not imply amnesia. When the Bible says that God "will remember their sins no more," it doesn't mean that He suddenly has no recollection of an offense. It means that God does not catalog our sins and use the information against us.

Forgiveness is NOT minimizing the hurt.

Forgiveness does not water down the offense by saying something like, "It's OK, it wasn't that bad," or "I know you didn't mean to hurt me." The truth is you've been hurt deeply and, perhaps, very intentionally. Forgiveness does not say, "I'm all right; it's just a flesh wound," when real trauma is involved. Instead, forgiveness calls the violation what it is just as an umpire calls what he sees.

Forgiveness does NOT necessarily mean reconciliation.

Perhaps you were thinking, "If I forgive the doctor, my ex-boyfriend, and my parents, then I have to initiate or at least be receptive to reconciliation." Truthfully, some of you already are open to reconciliation and would give anything for it to happen, but reconciliation isn't even on the radar screen of some of the people involved in your abortion. The thought of a required reconciliation feels like being sentenced to life in prison without parole. Forgiveness recognizes that reconciliation may be neither possible nor wise following the abortion. Forgiving someone doesn't require becoming best friends or even close acquaintances with him or her.

3. Do any of these definitions of what forgiveness is *not* alter your views about forgiveness? Do these qualifiers make you more open to forgiving those involved in your abortion? Why or why not?

FORGIVENESS IN ACTION

A wonderful story in the Bible tells about a young man who had every reason to hate and hold a grudge. He even had an opportunity to experience the joy of a "pay back," but he chose a different response. Joseph's story begins in Genesis 37 and goes for 10 chapters. (Before the next session, read the entire passage to let God show you the way to redemptive healing!) Joseph was favored by his father but alienated by his brothers. When he was only 17, his brothers actually sold him into slavery. According to God's plan, he ended up in the powerful kingdom of Egypt.

Joseph was later imprisoned for a crime he didn't commit and for 13 years faced shame and rejection. Through a series of divine interventions, Joseph left prison and became the second ruler of Egypt, reporting directly to Pharaoh. Ironically, he soon found himself with his brothers in great need of his help.

> LEADER: *Read Genesis 45:1-8 aloud. Discuss as many discovery questions as time permits. It will help to highlight in advance the questions you don't want to miss.*

¹ *Joseph could no longer keep his composure in front of all his attendants, so he called out, "Send everyone away from me!" No one was with him when he revealed his identity to his brothers.* ² *But he wept so loudly that the Egyptians heard it, and also Pharaoh's household heard it.* ³ *Joseph said to his brothers, "I am Joseph! Is my father still living?" But his brothers were too terrified to answer him.* ⁴ *Then Joseph said to his brothers, "Please, come near me," and they came near. "I am Joseph, your brother," he said, "the one you sold into Egypt.* ⁵ *And now don't be worried or angry with yourselves for selling me here, because God sent me ahead of you to preserve life.* ⁶ *For the famine has been in the land these two years, and there will be five more years without plowing or harvesting.* ⁷ *God sent me ahead of you to establish you as a remnant within the land and to keep you alive by a great deliverance.* ⁸ *Therefore it was not you who sent me here, but God. He has made me a father to Pharaoh, lord of his entire household, and ruler over all the land of Egypt."*

GENESIS 45:1-8, HCSB

4. Why, when they recognized Joseph, were the brothers terrified (verse 3)?

5. What perspective did Joseph display in verses 5-8 that enabled him to more easily forgive his brothers? Why does this perspective make such a difference?

6. Share a time when someone extended forgiveness to you that you knew you did not deserve. How did that feel? How did that act of forgiveness change you?

Joseph had every reason and opportunity to repay his brothers for the agony they caused him. Joseph, however, did not choose to take that opportunity. He forgave them because he'd allowed love to replace bitterness and because he'd learned the truth of Romans 8:28:

We know that God causes all things to work together for good to those who love God, to those who are called according to His purpose.

ROMANS 8:28, NASB

7. Does Romans 8:28 say, "God causes all things to happen"? What does it say God causes? How might this apply to our abortions and other past mistakes?

GOD'S VIEW OF FORGIVENESS

12 Since God chose you to be the holy people he loves, you must clothe yourselves with tenderhearted mercy, kindness, humility, gentleness, and patience. 13 Make allowance for each other's faults, and forgive anyone who offends you. Remember, the Lord forgave you, so you must forgive others. 14 Above all, clothe yourselves with love, which binds us all together in perfect harmony. 15 And let the peace that comes from Christ rule in your hearts. For as members of one body you are called to live in peace. And always be thankful.

COLOSSIANS 3:12-15, NLT

8. According to Colossians 3:13, what does God require of us? Does He give us the option to choose whom we'll forgive and whom we won't?

9. What motivation to forgive others are we given in verses 12-13? What do you think God expects of us when it comes to forgiving others?

10. Verses 14-15 highlight three godly traits that we need to put on like clothing. What are the traits and where do they come from? How strong are these traits in your life right now?

God commands forgiveness for our benefit. Forgiveness helps maintain harmony in relationships. It also creates deep peace and joy in the lives of the two captives it sets free—your offender and you!

Embracing the Truth

LEADER: During this "Embracing the Truth" time, we'll discuss the benefits of forgiveness and the consequences of not forgiving. We'll also explore the topic of accepting God's forgiveness. Forgiveness will not happen overnight; it's a process to which each one must commit if she is going to be free from the bondage of resentment and bitterness.

Right to Be Angry

As a woman who has faced the pain and loneliness of abortion, you have the right to be angry with many people—at the very least the lawmakers, media, and medical community whose responsibility it is to protect life and to ensure truth is provided. You have the right to be angry and to feel betrayed by some of your loved ones and your circumstances.

True forgiveness is seldom easy. It can be quite costly, but it's a powerful weapon for tearing down strongholds in our lives and hearts. The enemy uses unforgiveness and anger to keep us in bondage. When we surrender our unforgiveness and anger, we set our own hearts free so God can take us places we never dreamed possible.

1. A number of barriers can hinder a person from letting go of her anger, thus interfering with the healing process. Which of the following barriers to forgiveness apply to you?

- ❏ If I forgive the offender, he or she will never understand the severity of the act.
- ❏ If I forgive, I will look weak; I have my pride.
- ❏ He/she doesn't deserve forgiveness, only punishment. I can't let him/her off the hook.
- ❏ Forgiveness isn't possible for this (I believe abortion is unforgivable).
- ❏ The offender shows no remorse. I have no responsibility to forgive.
- ❏ If I let go of my anger, I may also let go of my child.
- ❏ Letting go of anger means letting go of my relationships with persons involved in the abortion (sometimes anger is the only emotion connecting people).
- ❏ I'm comfortable with the status quo, and I'm afraid of the unknowns that will come.
- ❏ Other: _____

Benefits and Consequences

We often believe the lie that our anger effectively punishes the offender. The truth is that it's we, in fact, who are imprisoned by it. Frederick Buechner writes in *Wishful Thinking*:

> *Of the Seven Deadly Sins, anger is possibly the most fun. To lick your wounds, to smack your lips over grievances long past, to roll over your tongue the prospect of bitter confrontations still to come,*

to savor to the last toothsome morsel both the pain you are given and the pain you are giving back—in many ways it is a feast fit for a king. The chief drawback is that what you are wolfing down is yourself. The skeleton at the feast is you. When we choose to forgive, we release our prisoner from the dungeon and discover that we are subsequently freed from the dank cell of our own bitterness. Spiritually and emotionally, forgiveness frees us. [1]

2. On a scale of 1 to 10, what would it mean to you to walk in the freedom of forgiveness?

1	2	3	4	5	6	7	8	9	10
I don't care!		I'm considering it.			It's tough, but I want it.			I'd pay any price.	

3. How has withholding forgiveness held you spiritually and emotionally captive?

4. In Genesis 50:20, Joseph told his brothers, "You intended to harm me, but God intended it for good to accomplish what is now being done, the saving of many lives" (NIV). Can you imagine yourself saying similar words? What prevents you from trusting that God can work even your abortion for some good in your life?

FORGIVING YOURSELF

It's common for post-abortive women to feel that while God has forgiven them, they need to forgive themselves. But the Bible never identifies the need to forgive ourselves. The key is not forgiving yourself but accepting God's forgiveness.

[8] *For by grace you are saved through faith, and this is not from yourselves; it is God's gift—* [9] *not from works, so that no one can boast.*

EPHESIANS 2:8-9, HCSB

[13] *He has rescued us from the domain of darkness and transferred us into the kingdom of the Son He loves,* [14] *in whom we have redemption, the forgiveness of sins.*

COLOSSIANS. 1:13-14, HCSB

In [Jesus] we have redemption through his blood, the forgiveness of sins, in accordance with the riches of God's grace.

EPHESIANS 1:7, NIV

5. According to Ephesians 2:8-9 and Colossians 1:23-24, who saves us, forgives us, and redeems us? If we merely forgive ourselves, have we truly been forgiven for our sin?

6. According to Ephesians 1:7 and 2:8-9, what can we do to earn forgiveness? What is the basis for God's forgiveness in our lives?

If we confess our sins, [God] is faithful and righteous to forgive us our sins and to cleanse us from all unrighteousness.

1 JOHN 1:9, HCSB

7. Only God can forgive our sins against Him, but what does He require of us? How difficult is it for you to confess sins to God, acknowledging your responsibility in them?

When we as Christ-followers say, "I know God can forgive me, but I can't forgive myself," we are elevating our ability to forgive over God's ability. True healing and freedom only occur when we can accept the forgiveness God so graciously wants to give each of us. In not completely accepting God's forgiveness, you're essentially buying the lie that Christ's sacrifice on the cross was not sufficient to cover your abortion.

CONNECTING

LEADERS: See the separate Leader Guide for powerful and visual exercises for use during the "Connecting" time.

We've been reminded that if we confess our sins, wounds, failures, and false beliefs to God, He'll forgive, renew, transform, restore, and redeem us. If you are in a group environment, your leader will share an exercise with you. If you are doing this study alone, sit with the Lord in a quiet place with worship music and ask Him to speak to you personally about His forgiveness.

1. What did you hear from God during this experience? What feelings did you have as the things you confessed disintegrated before your eyes?

LEADER INSTRUCTIONS FOR GROUP EXPERIENCE: *Instruct group members to pull out the two letters they wrote this past week for the "Taking Truth Home" assignment for session 4. Have members exchange and read aloud to the group only the one that was written to another woman as if from God.*

2. Exchange with another member the letter you wrote from God to a woman searching for abortion healing. Take turns reading these letters aloud. Write today's date on the letter and keep it in your Bible as a remembrance of forgiving others and receiving God's forgiveness. Once you have confessed and been forgiven, consider the case closed. If you are not in a group, consider sharing this letter with your prayer partner.

Pray with one another about the things that have been mentioned in the group's letters.

MY PRAYER AND SUPPORT NEEDS

MY GROUP'S PRAYER AND SUPPORT NEEDS

Taking Truth Home

Questions to Take to My Heart

Look into your heart for the answers to these questions. This is introspection time—time to grapple with what drives your thinking and behavior. Every action has a corresponding belief that drives it. Remember, the Devil is the true villain in the story; he wants to keep you stuck where you are, robbing you of your joy and closure. Be sure to journal your thoughts, struggles, and insights.

✴ Which people or organizations am I still struggling to forgive? What lies am I holding onto about God, other people, or myself that are blocking God's healing work in my life and in the lives of others?

Journal Exercise

Read the following excerpt entitled "At the Foot of the Cross," written by a fellow Surrendering Sister:[2]

Understanding the cross is the key to true forgiveness and freedom. Imagine what it might have been like for Jesus in the garden of Gethsemane. He agonized for you and me, His soul in anguish for the sins of the world. It causes me to reflect on the weight and burden of my own personal sins. The sins of just one person alone can be smothering; we know that as post-abortive women. The sin can emotionally paralyze us or spiritually blind us. Our own set of burdens can lead to the death of our souls. Our human strength cannot shoulder such a burden—we would be crushed.

At Gethsemane Jesus was given a vision of the sin of the entire world, including yours and mine—past, present and future. Knowing what a burden your own sin has been to carry, imagine the weight of all the world's sin!

God, our loving Father, knew there was only one man who could bear the entire burden, endure the overwhelming spiritual agony, and nail it all to the cross once and for all. For us there is only one hope.

Mary Magdalene knew that hope. She touched the feet of Jesus and was forgiven. Mary Magdalene also watched as Jesus carried her sin all the way to the cross. He bore what she could not. He endured the emotional, physical, and spiritual torment of sin.

This sin presented itself as an angry crowd judging and insulting. He beheld the shame, anger, unforgiveness, and every other emotion that separates us from God. He did not leave one sin behind.

At the end of the journey, as Jesus is nailed to the cross, so is your every sin. The screaming shame of abortion is silenced by the agony of our Lord as His hands are nailed to the cross. The loneliness and rejection are thorns in the crown upon His head. His pierced side pours out His blood that covers the agony of our hearts and cleanses our souls and minds.

With the last words spoken, "It is finished," we are reminded that our burden of sin has been fully lifted. A great cost was paid for our forgiveness—a huge price for us to be reconciled to God.

Your Fellow Surrendering Sister

Take time to reflect as if you were Mary Magdalene standing at the foot of the cross. Journal your thoughts about what you have read this week. Receive your gifts of forgiveness, healing, and peace. Your debt is paid in full, the accuser is silenced, and you are set free.

NOTES

1. Frederick Buechner, *Wishful Thinking*, (San Francisco, Harper, 1993)
2. Used by permission.

At the Foot of the Cross

Pat's Journal Entry 6

Tears welled up from the depths of my soul, and it felt as if they'd never stop. That night of sobbing in the bathtub was a major turning point for me. The truth of what I had done to my child had finally sunk into my heart, and the grief overwhelmed me. Abortion had taken so much from me! I grieved over my sinful choices, the struggles in my life, my wounded heart, and, most of all, my precious baby.

After 33 years of carrying the burden myself, I finally gave my sin to God. I thought I'd already done that at the ladies retreat, but I'd stopped short. What I had given there was my broken life—my marriage, my emotions, my needs, and my expectations. I gave what I knew to give. The night in the bathtub, however, I faced the cross. For the first time, I understood the sin that Jesus had personally carried to the cross for me. I understood the darkness of my heart at a level far beyond my personal needs. I understood that I could not save myself, that I needed a rescuer. Not until that night did I grasp the amazing depth of my Rescuer's love for me.

As I cried, I washed as though I could wash away all the dirt and pain of my life. In truth, I scrubbed at my body the way a rape victim tries to wash away the violent invasion of rape. As I bathed, I grasped the meaning of the cross at a deeper level and gratefully accepted the sacrifice of the cross. I understood that Jesus Christ willingly gave His life for mine—to set me free, to heal me, and to redeem my entire life.

Gradually, the tears for my own loss transformed into tears for the incredible burden that Jesus took on Himself and the passionate love that drove Him to shoulder it. My burden was more than I could bear, but He bore the burden of every person on the planet.

While I began the night releasing tears, I ended it by releasing my grip on my sins, my hurts, and my burdens. A year earlier at the ladies retreat, I surrendered my head. That night in the bathtub, I surrendered my heart.

The cleansing I felt was amazing! It was wonderful! It still is.

FROM GRIEF TO THE GREAT EXCHANGE

BREAKING THE ICE

LEADER: Use this time to allow members to share some feeling from this past week. The following questions will help group members focus on wonderful gifts and exchanges. Show video for session 6 (optional).

1. What's one of the most expensive no-strings-attached gifts you've ever received? How did it feel to receive such a gift?

2. If you could trade in anything old in your life for something brand new at no cost to you, what would it be? Explain.

3. Take a few minutes to reflect on what God has brought you through. Make a list of some emotions, behaviors, or character traits that you brought with you into this study. It could be something you struggle with such as anger, fear, insecurity, or relationship issues. It could be feelings of loss or anger. As you jot these down, ask God to use this session to help you to exchange these old things and feelings in your life for a new thing, a new emotion, or a new character trait.

Opening Prayer

Lord, thank You for giving me eyes to see and ears to hear all that You have for me in this session. Even when I don't fully understand Your ways, I know You truly want what's best for me. I want to receive everything You have for me and give everything that I have to You. Help my understanding Lord, and lead me into the truth and healing that You long for me to experience. I desire to honor and serve You. Show me the way, God. I have lived with my secrets for so long I am tired of trying to be something I am not. Most of the people closest to me don't have a clue about my past. But I know. You know. Lord, I am tired of living a double life. Please help me understand and embrace the new life You have for me. Draw me close. Heal me. Set me free!

Objectives for this Session

- Discover the difference between godly sorrow and destructive sorrow
- Understand how God changes us from the inside out
- Learn to address past wounds by embracing our pain and rejecting our shame
- Understand the process of change, healing, and wholeness
- Accept that we're new creations in Christ, with new hearts and hope for a new future

Discovering the Truth

LEADER: *In "Discovering the Truth," you will discover two kinds of sorrow that are discussed in the Bible.*

Last week we made great progress in our journey toward forgiving those involved in our abortions. We also began to understand and accept God's forgiveness for us. The path of forgiveness is intertwined with the path of grieving. As our losses from abortion become more real to us, we will grieve more deeply and, in that grief, we'll need to revisit the step of forgiveness. As we move together to step 6 on our map, we'll focus on the importance of grieving our losses and receiving God's gift of wholeness.

MY HEALING JOURNEY

SHARING THE
SECRET: A SPRING
IN THE
DESERT

WHERE HAVE
YOU COME
FROM?

WALK IN
TRUTH

A TIME FOR ANGER:
TEARING DOWN
ROADBLOCKS

FORGIVENESS:
A GIANT STEP
TOWARD
FREEDOM

FROM GRIEF
TO THE GREAT
EXCHANGE

TWO KINDS OF SORROW

Any traumatic event in our lives will create sorrow. Many people experience deep sorrow that leads to depression, addictions, and a host of other dark places of the soul.

Grieving does not have to be destructive. God gave us the gift of grieving as a way to deal with life's difficulties and disappointments. The apostle Paul explained the difference between two kinds of sorrow in his second letter to the Corinthian church:

[9] *Now I'm glad—not that you were upset, but that you were jarred into turning things around. You let the distress bring you to God, not drive you from him. The result was all gain, no loss.* [10] *Distress that drives us to God ... turns us around. It gets us back in the way of salvation. We never regret that kind of pain. But those who let distress drive them away from God are full of regrets, and end up on a deathbed of regrets.* [11] *And now, isn't it wonderful all the ways in which this distress has goaded you closer to God? You're more alive, more concerned, more sensitive, more reverent, more human, more passionate, more responsible. Looked at from this angle, you've come out of this with purity of heart.*

2 CORINTHIANS 7:9-11, THE MESSAGE

1. How did Paul differentiate between godly distress/sorrow and destructive distress/sorrow (vv. 9-10)?

2. What's the end result of destructive sorrow? What's the end result of godly sorrow?

In past sessions, we discovered the importance of replacing lies—false beliefs we've embraced—with truth from God. If we'll allow our pain and sorrow to drive us toward God rather than away from Him, we'll experience transformation, healing, and new life.

Because past memories, sorrow, and hurts are uncomfortable for us, we try to avoid them or find ways to escape the pain. And yet, Paul was happy about the Corinthians' struggles and distress because it jarred them into change. Jesus also promoted godly sorrow and gave those who are hurting a wonderful promise:

Blessed are those who mourn, because they will be comforted.

MATTHEW 5:4, HCSB

3. What did Jesus promise in Matthew 5:4 to those who are willing to remember their wounds and stay in their pain? Why is remembering and grieving our losses and failures so vital in healing from hurts and traumas?

OUR TRUSTWORTHY GUIDE

As we're truly open about our feelings with God, He'll take us further down the path to healing. Most of us, though, have doubts about God's goodness and, specifically, about His heart toward us personally. Let's see what God says about us.

¹ Do not be afraid, for I have ransomed you. I have called you by name; you are mine. ² When you go through deep waters, I will be with you. When you go through rivers of difficulty, you will not drown. When you walk through the fire of oppression, you will not be burned up; the flames will not consume you. ³ For I am the LORD, your God, the Holy One of Israel, your Savior.

ISAIAH 43:1B-3A, NLT

¹¹ On that day you will not be put to shame for all the wrongs you have done to me, because I will remove from this city those who rejoice in their pride. Never again will you be haughty on my holy hill. ¹² But I will leave within you the meek and humble, who trust in the name of the LORD … ¹⁵ The LORD has taken away your punishment, he has turned back your enemy. The LORD, the King of Israel, is with you; never again will you fear any harm. … ¹⁷ The LORD your God is with you, he is mighty to save. He will take great delight in you, he will quiet you with his love, he will rejoice over you with singing."

ZEPHANIAH 3:11-12,15,17, NIV

4. What assurances did God give in Isaiah 43:1-3 for the various fears we might face? Which of these assurances gives you the greatest comfort? Explain.

5. God promised that He won't put His children to shame (Zeph. 3:11) and will take away our punishment (Zeph. 3:15). What vital heart attitudes does God identify in verse 12 that we must embrace to be saved?

6. What does Zephaniah 3:17 tell you about God's heart toward you personally? How does it make you feel when you hear that God takes "great delight in you" and "rejoices over you with singing"?

7. What's the worst thing that could happen as you face your fears and allow God to take you back into your pain and losses? What could this group do to help you risk the next step you know you need to take?

Fear is often the greatest enemy to meaningful life change. We long to return to what's familiar rather than take risks and face the unknown. More than anything else, the healing journey requires us to trust God. Healing the wounds in our innermost being will lead us down paths we never could have imagined. So we take one day and one step at a time as we walk into the shadows with Jesus, allow Him to turn the shadows to light, to ease our pain, and then to lead us into freedom, truth, and the true desires of our hearts.

EMBRACING THE TRUTH

LEADER: In the initial part of "Embracing the Truth," you'll discuss the process of repentance—change from the inside out. Then you'll focus on what it means to be a new creation in Christ.

We have already focused on the vital step of grieving our losses. The next step in our journey will open our minds and hearts to the incredible vistas that await us at the summit of our climb. We are more than we've become and more than we realize. It's time to make the great exchange—to accept who we really are *in Christ*.

CHANGE FROM THE INSIDE OUT

God's forgiveness, which comes with our confession, is a very powerful force in our lives. God's blessings don't stop when we receive salvation. He wants to help us really change. That happens through our repentance. Unfortunately, that word has been given a bad connotation over the years. *Repent* comes from the Greek word *metanoia*, which means to change (*meta*) our mind-set or understanding (*noia*). The word *metamorphosis* is a related term, meaning a change in form or substance, and is used to describe what occurs when a caterpillar retreats into its cocoon to emerge as a butterfly. This is a wondrous thing, but God does even more wondrous things for His children.

²¹ "Pay attention, O Jacob, for you are my servant, O Israel. I, the LORD, made you, and I will not forget you. ²² I have swept away your sins like a cloud. I have scattered your offenses like the morning mist. Oh, return to me, for I have paid the price to set you free." ²³ Sing, O heavens, for the LORD has done this wondrous thing. Shout for joy, O depths of the earth! Break into song, O mountains and forests and every tree! For the LORD has redeemed Jacob and is glorified in Israel.

ISAIAH 44:21-23, NLT

1. God's words in Isaiah 44 apply to the history of Israel, but they also give us an excellent starting place for our repentance. According to verses 21-22, what "wondrous things" does God accomplish for us? What is our choice and part in the process?

¹ I urge you, brothers, in view of God's mercy, to offer your bodies as living sacrifices, holy and pleasing to God —this is your spiritual act of worship. ² Do not conform any longer to the pattern of this world, but be transformed by the renewing of your mind. Then you will be able to test and approve what God's will is —His good, pleasing, and perfect will.

ROMANS 12:1-2, NIV

³¹ Jesus said … "If you continue in My word, you really are My disciples. ³² You will know the truth, and the truth will set you free."

JOHN 8:31-32, HCSB

2. Romans 12:1-2 and John 8:31-32 also separate the process of repentance or transformation into God's part and our part. What is God's part and what is ours?

As we turn to God and begin to give Him our secrets, our shame, false beliefs, and distorted perspectives, we become engaged in a battle of the mind and heart. Recall the model we discussed in session 2 in which our wounds become infected with lies that lead to destructive agreements and a false sense of self.

³ For though we live in the world, we do not wage war as the world does. ⁴ The weapons we fight with are not the weapons of the world. On the contrary, they have divine power to demolish strongholds. ⁵ We demolish arguments and every pretension that sets itself up against the knowledge of God, and we take captive every thought to make it obedient to Christ.

2 CORINTHIANS 10:3-5, NIV

3. According to 2 Corinthians 10:5, where is the cosmic battle between good and evil waged? What "strongholds" must we demolish in this battle?

4. In 2 Corinthians 10:4-5, Paul talked about demolishing "strongholds." Imagine castles and fortified strongholds. What would it take to demolish them? What kind of battle and reconstruction process would demolish the lies and distortions that hold us captive?

As we recognize the battle being waged over our minds and hearts, it becomes clearer why change must occur from the inside out, beginning in our innermost being—our hearts and minds. It is God who transforms us. Our part in repentance is to persistently decide to turn or return to God.

GRIEVING OUR LOSSES

God sees your pain, your losses, your shame. He not only gives you permission to grieve your losses, but He invites you to grieve. Grief is the process God created to help us deal with the inevitable losses of life. As you come to grips with the things abortion has taken away from you, then you can leave it at Jesus' feet—"where Grace and mercy meet." God longs to comfort you and to set you free so your can lift your head.

5. Take some quiet time by yourself as your leader directs. In the space provided, begin to write down some of your losses—those things, opportunities, people, relationships, experiences, or feelings that abortion either has taken away from you or never allowed you to experience.

When instructed by your leader, close your eyes and imagine Jesus walking into the room, putting His arms around you, and gently speaking these words to you:

[1] *Do not be afraid, for I have ransomed you. I have called you by name; you are mine.* [2] *When you go through deep waters, I will be with you. When you go through rivers of difficulty, you will not drown. When you walk through the fire of oppression, you will not be burned up; the flames will not consume you* [3] *For I am the LORD, your God, the Holy One of Israel, your Savior.*

ISAIAH 43:1B-3A, NLT

In last week's assignment, you walked through an exercise called, "At the Foot of the Cross." At this point in your journey, it's important to understand what happened with Jesus at the cross. True and lasting freedom only comes as we understand the ransom price Jesus paid for our freedom, and as we accept His payment as our only hope of salvation and real life. If you have questions about accepting Jesus' sacrifice and free gift of eternal salvation, please see your group leader after the session.

STEPS TO THE CROSS

1) God created you and loves you. (Genesis 1:26-27; John 3:16-18)

2) We've fallen from our original glory. (Genesis 3:1,13; Romans 3:23)

3) Jesus came to rescue you from darkness and captivity. (Colossians 1:12-14)

4) Jesus is your only hope for abundant and eternal life. (John 14:6)

5) You must choose life. (John 1:12-13; John 5:24)

ALL THINGS NEW

Too often we see ourselves as the sum of all our failures. We get blinded to who we really are and how God sees us after we've placed our trust in Jesus to rescue and redeem us.

17 Therefore, if anyone is in Christ, he is a new creation; the old has gone, the new has come! 18 All this is from God, who reconciled us to himself through Christ and gave us the ministry of reconciliation.
2 CORINTHIANS 5:17-18, NIV

[God foretelling about the New Covenant in Jesus:]
25 I will sprinkle clean water on you, and you will be clean; I will cleanse you from all your filthiness and from all your idols. 26 Moreover, I will give you a new heart and put a new spirit within you; and I will remove the heart of stone from your flesh and give you a heart of flesh. 27 I will put my Spirit within you and cause you to walk in My statutes, and you will be careful to follow My ordinances. ... 28 you will be My people, and I will be your God.
EZEKIEL 36:25-28, NASB

6. Who, according to 2 Corinthians 5:17-18, becomes a "new creation"? What has happened to the old things (our desires, inclinations, nature)?

7. According to Ezekiel 36:25-28, what key changes does God make in our lives when we become new creations in Christ?

8. If Christians become new and have new hearts and spirits, then why do we still sometimes feel at the mercy of "idols" (Ezekiel 36:25)—God substitutes?

Amazingly, God makes us entirely new creations when we place our faith in Jesus. The only problem is that most of us never experience much of this "new creation." Why?

- The enemy continues to deceive us, telling us God doesn't care and that we're nothing.
- We continue to live out of the well-worn patterns and ruts in our lives and don't embrace our new hearts and new lives.
- We block the work of the Holy Spirit by resisting Him or turning away from God, going our own way, and seeking satisfaction apart from Him.

YOUR FAVORED POSITION IN GOD'S FAMILY

God's love is lavished on those who place their faith in Jesus. Because of nothing other than God's extreme love for us, we've been given a position that few of us have grasped, and even fewer live in. Our enemy clearly wants to keep this hidden.

[14] All those led by God's Spirit are God's sons. [15] For you did not receive a spirit of slavery to fall back into fear, but you received the Spirit of adoption, by whom we cry out, "Abba, Father!" [16] The Spirit Himself testifies together with our spirit that we are God's children, [17] and if children, also heirs—heirs of God and co-heirs with Christ —seeing that we suffer with Him so that we may also be glorified with Him.

ROMANS 8:14-17, HCSB

[1] If you have been raised up with Christ, keep seeking the things above, where Christ is, seated at the right hand of God. [2] Set your mind on the things above, not on the things that are on earth. [3] For you have died and your life is hidden with Christ in God. [4] When Christ, who is our life, is revealed, then you also will be revealed with Him in glory.

COLOSSIANS 3:1-4, NASB

9. What amazing privileges do each of us receive when we become children of God, with the full status of a firstborn son (Romans 8:14-17; COLOSSIANS 3:1-4)?

We've already been granted the privileges of the firstborn, but our position as royalty won't be fully revealed until Jesus returns in His glory. We participate spiritually in His death, resurrection, and glorification. We're daughters of the King of kings, co-heirs with Christ!

10. How might embracing our favored status affect the way we approach life, the enemy, and our enslavement to past sins and failures (Romans 8:15,17; COLOSSIANS 3:2-3)?

TRADING SORROWS FOR JOY

The Bible is full of prophecies and promises that God will fulfill in part now and to the fullest extent when Jesus comes to take us into His eternal kingdom. Jeremiah 31 gives us one of these exciting prophecies for Israel, which also applies to Christ-followers under the New Covenant:

¹² *They will come home and sing songs of joy on the heights of Jerusalem. They will be radiant because of the LORD's good gifts—the abundant crops of grain, new wine, and olive oil, and the healthy flocks and herds. Their life will be like a watered garden, and all their sorrows will be gone.* ¹³ *The young women will dance for joy, and the men—old and young—will join in the celebration. I will turn their mourning into joy. I will comfort them and exchange their sorrow for rejoicing.* ¹⁴ *The priests will enjoy abundance, and my people will feast on my good gifts. I, the LORD, have spoken!"*

JEREMIAH 31:12-14, NLT

11. In your own words, how would you describe the scene pictured in Jeremiah 31:12-14? Although our current lives will still have troubles, what has God given us that should lead us to rejoice?

12. What's the exchange highlighted in verse 13? Do you believe God can make this exchange happen in your life now?

CONNECTING

OUR CAPTIVE HEARTS

God has an adventure waiting for us as we begin to accept and appreciate who we really are and who He really is. The villain in our story continues to feed us lies about God's goodness and also about our value to God. He wants to keep us enslaved and ineffective. But we're now wise to this scheme; we know the truth: Jesus brings amazing hope to all the hurting and captives. Jesus quoted Isaiah 61 to describe His mission in our world.

¹The Spirit of the Sovereign LORD is on me, because the LORD has anointed me to preach good news to the poor. He has sent me to bind up the brokenhearted, to proclaim freedom for the captives and release from darkness for the prisoners, ² to proclaim the year of the LORD's favor and the day of vengeance of our God, to comfort all who mourn, ³ and provide for those who grieve in Zion—to bestow on them a crown of beauty instead of ashes, the oil of gladness instead of mourning, and a garment of praise instead of a spirit of despair. They will be called oaks of righteousness, a planting of the LORD for the display of his splendor. ⁴ They will rebuild the ancient ruins and restore the places long devastated; they will renew the ruined cities that have been devastated for generations. ... ⁷ Instead of their shame my people will receive a double portion, and instead of disgrace they will rejoice in their inheritance; and so they will inherit a double portion in their land, and everlasting joy will be theirs.

ISAIAH 61:1-4, 7, NIV

1. Consider the following list of issues from Isaiah 61, and rate the presence of each characteristic in your life.

	Can't Identify									Definitely Present
Brokenhearted	1	2	3	4	5	6	7	8	9	10
Captive	1	2	3	4	5	6	7	8	9	10
Darkness	1	2	3	4	5	6	7	8	9	10
Mourning	1	2	3	4	5	6	7	8	9	10
Burned ashes	1	2	3	4	5	6	7	8	9	10
Grieving	1	2	3	4	5	6	7	8	9	10
Despair	1	2	3	4	5	6	7	8	9	10
Ruins	1	2	3	4	5	6	7	8	9	10
Devastation	1	2	3	4	5	6	7	8	9	10
Shame	1	2	3	4	5	6	7	8	9	10
Disgrace	1	2	3	4	5	6	7	8	9	10

THE GREAT EXCHANGE

Paradise will come only when Jesus returns to take us into glory. He too longs for that day when He can be fully united with His people—His bride. But even now Jesus offers freedom from our captivity and amazing gifts if we will but embrace them.

I delight greatly in the LORD; my soul rejoices in my God. For he has clothed me with garments of salvation and arrayed me in a robe of righteousness, as a bridegroom adorns his head like a priest, and as a bride adorns herself with her jewels.

ISAIAH 61:10, NIV

2. Look at the Isaiah 61 list again, but focus this time on the promises and good gifts God gives to replace life's bad stuff. Draw a line to connect each of the negative attributes on the left side with its corresponding positive one on the right.

Brokenhearted	Freedom
Mourning	Crown of beauty
Darkness	Provision
Grieving	Rebuilding
Disgrace	Praise
Despair	Healing
Ruins	Comfort and gladness
Shame	Double portion of blessing
Devastation	Light
Captive	Rejoicing/Joy
Burned ashes	Restoration

3. Circle the negative characteristics you most need to exchange for their positive counterparts. Share with your prayer partner or group the items you circled.

LEADER: *As each woman shares her exchange needs in question 3, pause to pray, asking God to replace that hurt with the blessing He promises.*

It's often difficult to grasp that the only reason Jesus sacrificed Himself was for you—He loves *you*! In John 10:10 He says, "I have come that they may have life and have it to the full."

4. Take a moment and write out John 10:10, but put your name in place of "they."

By now, if not before, you have clearly recognized and accepted Jesus as your personal Savior. It's time to fully capture all He desires for your life. Will you put your shattered dreams, your hopes, your past, present, and future—your whole heart—in His hands?

Taking Truth Home

Grieving your child is something your mother's heart has longed to do. At this point in our journey, stop punishing yourself and give yourself permission to grieve. You've been forgiven and God is ever at your side. It's time for a difficult, but wonderfully healing step!

Your Letter
This week write a letter (or poem or song) to your unborn child or children. *If you haven't taken time for any other homework, please make time for this one.* This is our opportunity to say all the things to our unborn child we've never said. We've spent a lot of time thinking about the abortion, now we have time to think about our sons or daughters.

Find a quiet place, and ask the Holy Spirit to give you revelation and direction. You may be surprised to find the sex of your child is revealed to you. Many women also report learning, in prayer, the name of their child (interestingly, not usually a name they'd have chosen).

If God does not reveal a name to you, then select one. Naming and connecting with our children gives them dignity and a chance for us to love them. We will find ourselves in love with our children, not angry about abortions. As you write, let go of the abortion experience; embrace God's love and presence. Use page 98 or your own paper.

Required Project for Session 7
For our next meeting, bring a flower that makes you think of your unborn child or allows others to remember him or her. Bring a separate flower for each of your unborn children.

Reminders of Who You Really Are
The "Who Am I?" reflections on page 99 are a great reminder whenever you need a boost to your spirits. Keep it handy and review it often.

Pray for the losses that each woman in the group has experienced, and invite Jesus to walk through the deep waters with each one. Ask God to begin even now to comfort, to restore, to redeem, and to pour out His love on the members of this group.

LEADER: Two key points: (1) Emphasize that you and any other leaders would love to talk with anyone who has questions about a personal relationship with Jesus or receiving the salvation Jesus offers. (2) Highlight the simple but important special project included in the "Taking Truth Home" section that's required preparation for session 7.

MY PRAYER AND SUPPORT NEEDS

MY GROUP'S PRAYER AND SUPPORT NEEDS

FROM MOMMY ...

WHO AM I?*

I renounce the lie that I am rejected, unloved, dirty, or shameful, because in Christ I am *COMPLETELY accepted*. GOD SAYS ...

John 1:12	*I am God's child.*
John 15:5	*I am Christ's friend.*
Romans 5:1	*I have been justified.*
I Corinthians 6:17	*I am united with the Lord and I am one spirit with Him.*
I Corinthians 6:19-20	*I have been bought with a price. I belong to God.*
I Corinthians 12:27	*I am a member of Christ's body.*
Ephesians 1:1	*I am a saint, a holy one.*
Ephesians 1:5	*I have been adopted as God's child.*
Ephesians 2:18	*I have direct access to God through the Holy Spirit.*
Colossians 1:14	*I have been redeemed and forgiven of all my sins.*
Colossians 2:10	*I am complete in Christ.*

I renounce the lie that I am guilty, unprotected, alone, or abandoned because IN CHRIST I am *TOTALLY secure*. GOD SAYS ...

Romans 8:1-2	*I am free forever from condemnation.*
Romans 8:28	*I am assured all things work together for good.*
Romans 8:31-34	*I am free from any condemning charges against me.*
Romans 8:35-39	*I cannot be separated from the love of God.*
Corinthians 1:21-22	*I have been established, anointed, and sealed by God.*
Philippians 1:6	*I am confident that the good work God has begun in me will be perfected.*
Colossians 3:3	*I am hidden with Christ in God.*
2 Timothy 1:7	*I have not been given a spirit of fear, but of power, love, and a sound mind.*
Hebrews 4:16	*I can find grace and mercy to help in time of need.*
I John 5:18	*I am born of God and the evil one cannot touch me.*

I renounce the lie that I am worthless, inadequate, helpless, or hopeless because IN CHRIST I am *DEEPLY significant*. GOD SAYS...

Matthew 5:13-14	*I am the salt of the earth and the light of the world.*
John 15:1-5	*I am a branch of the true vine and a channel of His life*
John 15:16	*I have been chosen and appointed by God to bear fruit.*
Acts 1:8	*I am a personal, Spirit-empowered witness of Christ's.*
I Corinthians 3:16	*I am a temple of God.*
2 Corinthians 5:17-21	*I am a minister of reconciliation for God.*
Ephesians 2:6	*I am seated with Christ in the heavenly realm.*
Ephesians 2:10	*I am God's workmanship, created for good works.*
Ephesians 3:12	*I may approach God with freedom and confidence.*
Philippians 4:13	*I can do all things through Christ who gives me strength.*

*Adapted from Neil Anderson, *Living Free in Christ*, (Regal Books, 1993)

Who I Am in Christ

Rewrite some of the Who AM I? statements with your name inserted.

Consider what God has done for you and spend some quiet time with Him. Then write a prayer to Him expressing your heart.

Pat's Journal Entry 7

All my life, I've been an avid reader and writer. To chronicle my healing journey and pour out my feelings, I've kept a daily prayer journal for over 20 years. A large stash of yellowing, spiral-bound notebooks reside under my bed. I have no idea what I want to happen to them when I go home with Jesus. They're so very personal, telling the story of one broken woman rescued by one mighty God. Overflowing with wonderful testimonies of God's grace, they're also full of very selfish feelings, silliness, and lots of whining. But in the days of those early entries, I also took my first journeys through God's Word. Even then, He always answered my questions clearly and pointedly. I remember the day God showed me Psalm 139:13–16:

> [13] You made all the delicate, inner parts of my body and knit me together in my mother's womb. [14] Thank you for making me so wonderfully complex! Your workmanship is marvelous—how well I know it. [15] You watched me as I was being formed in utter seclusion, as I was woven together in the dark of the womb. [16] You saw me before I was born. Every day of my life was recorded in your book. Every moment was laid out before a single day had passed. (NLT)

My heart dropped as my mind envisioned my aborted child. Grief overwhelmed me. Although I knew God had forgiven my sin, I experienced new feelings of pain and loss as I realized how He felt about my baby—about every baby. Tears flowed from every cavern of my soul. I dropped to my bedroom floor with my head buried in my arms, crying out to God in sorrow and the emptiness of significant loss. As I cried, the Lord placed a vision in my mind's eye of little girl in a frilly pink dress. She was beautiful with long blonde hair; her arms stretched out to me as she smiled and said, "It's OK Mommy; I am happy here with Jesus. I forgive you and love you. I'll be here waiting when you come, but Jesus has some things for you to do first."

SHARING THE SECRET: A SPRING IN THE DESERT

THE PEACE OF RELEASE

A TIME FOR ANGER: TEARING DOWN ROADBLOCKS

FROM GRI TO THE GRI EXCHANG

WALK IN TRUTH

WHERE HAVE YOU COME FROM?

FORGIVENESS: A GIANT STEP TOWARD FREEDOM

THE PEACE OF RELEASE

OBJECTIVES FOR THIS SESSION

- To understand the peace and release found in surrendering our children to God
- To embrace support and freedom in sharing the loss of our unborn child and claiming their preciousness to God
- To experience the peace and healing that come with closure

SPECIAL MEMORIAL SERVICE

LEADER: This will be a unique and meaningful time for the members of your group. Make it special and memorable. You know your group best, so feel free to adjust the suggested structure of the service to fit the needs and personality of your group. Be sure to welcome everyone, and encourage them that this will be a special time. The separate Leader Guide contains detailed instructions for this special time. Show video for session 7 (optional).

NOTE: You will hear some participants on the video telling about receiving a vision for which they asked God. Note that they asked for a vision for very specific purpose but not for new Scripture from Him. Even though God reveals information to some participants, He loves all individuals whether or not they receive such a revelation. God speaks to all of us through Scripture and prayer.

WORDS OF TRUTH

Finally, we are going to allow ourselves to do what our hearts have desired to do for a long time. God has led you to this place. He has held you and comforted you through each step of this very difficult journey. He has embraced you in His arms as you have cried and stomped and grieved. He is with you now as He leads you and helps you to acknowledge your grief and to say good-bye to the child you have lost. We are truly at a crucial and special place in our healing journeys. This is the place where we can see our wounds healed, our broken hearts mended, and true reconciliation with our children accomplished. This is where God wants us to trade bondage for freedom, fear for courage, and shame for enduring joy.

This will not only be a time of closure but also a time of remembrance and of new beginnings as well as an enlightened opportunity to choose life! Throughout this memorial service, remember that you are God's child and are deeply loved by your Father. As you continue to embrace the loss of your child, you are free to mourn, to be comforted, and to comfort others who know the same pain that you have suffered.

If you are part of a healing group, you will be offered an opportunity at your next meeting to share your letter to your child. If you are doing the study alone, begin thinking about sharing your letter with your prayer partner. Spend some time asking God to prepare your heart for this sharing time.

✳ How did it feel to acknowledge your son or daughter as a child rather than a secret?

Opening Prayer

Lord, I thank You for Your grace. I thank You that You work all things together for good for those who love You. I thank You for the deeper personal relationship that I now have with You. In my weakness I have found Your strength. I pray that You will place the desire in my heart to share this journey with other women and to reach out to them as You have reached out to me, sharing the freedom and joy that You have secured for us.

Discovering the Truth

Who I am in Christ

Read "Who Am I?" on page 99 and allow these truths to seep into your heart.

Listen to these promises from God about your pain and your loss:

[17] *Your God is present among you, a strong Warrior there to save you. Happy to have you back, he'll calm you with his love and delight you with his songs.* [18] *"The accumulated sorrows of your exile will dissipate. I, your God, will get rid of them for you. You've carried those burdens long enough.* [19] *At the same time, I'll get rid of all those who've made your life miserable. I'll heal the maimed; I'll bring home the homeless. In the very countries where they were hated they will be venerated.* [20] *On Judgment Day I'll bring you back home—a great family gathering! You'll be famous and honored all over the world. You'll see it with your own eyes—all those painful partings turned into reunions!"*

ZEPHANIAH 3:17-20, THE MESSAGE

Listen to God's plan for your future:

⁵ *Trust in the* L*ORD* *with all your heart, and do not rely on your own understanding;* ⁶ *think about Him in all your ways, and He will guide you on the right paths.*

PROVERBS 3:5-6, HCSB

¹¹ *"For I know the plans I have for you," declares the* L*ORD, "plans to prosper you and not to harm you, plans to give you hope and a future.* ¹² *Then you will call upon me and come and pray to me, and I will listen to you.* ¹³ *You will seek me and find me when you seek me with all your heart.*

JEREMIAH 29:11-13, NIV

Listen to what Jesus has done with your past failures and sins:

⁴ *Surely our griefs He Himself bore, and our sorrows He carried; yet we ourselves esteemed Him stricken, smitten of God, and afflicted.* ⁵ *But He was pierced through for our transgressions, He was crushed for our iniquities; the chastening for our well-being fell upon Him, and by His scourging we are healed.*

ISAIAH 53:4-5, NASB

Read in unison these verses from Psalm 103:

² *Let all that I am praise the* L*ORD; may I never forget the good things he does for me.* ³ *He forgives all my sins and heals all my diseases.* ⁴ *He redeems me from death and crowns me with love and tender mercies. ...* ¹¹ *For his unfailing love toward those who fear him is as great as the height of the heavens above the earth.* ¹² *He has removed our sins as far from us as the east is from the west.* ¹³ *The* L*ORD is like a father to his children, tender and compassionate to those who fear him.*

PSALM 103:2-4,11-13, NLT

Jesus wants to encourage you as He did the disciples:

¹ *"Don't let your hearts be troubled. Trust in God, and trust also in me.* ² *There is more than enough room in my Father's home. If this were not so, would I have told you that I am going to prepare a place for you?* ³ *When everything is ready, I will come and get you, so that you will always be with me where I am.* ⁴ *And you know the way to where I am going."* ⁵ *"No, we don't know, Lord," Thomas said. "We have no idea where you are going, so how can we know the way?"* ⁶ *Jesus told him, "I am the way, the truth, and the life. No one can come to the Father except through me."*

JOHN 14:1-6, NLT

Prayer

God, this journey we're all taking together has been difficult and, at times, painful. Even so, we would do it again to receive the healing and grace that You are pouring over our lives. We have come to know You, ourselves, and our children in new and deeper ways. Let Your Spirit fill this place. Tonight, this is holy ground.

Embracing the Truth

Life ...

Remember that we have settled many truths about what the Bible has to say about life:

- Not only is your child fully human from the moment of conception, but he or she has already been given a personal, eternal soul.
- All prenatal existence is linked to a postnatal life. The life of our soul is an eternal spiritual continuum that begins at conception and continues into eternity.
- God placed inestimable value on your child from the moment of conception; he or she was created and deeply loved by God.
- At death, the unborn child immediately passes into the presence of God. Each of those little ones is present with the Father. They have identity and individuality; they deserve to be known for what they are: eternal beings. They still have a divine purpose which, though it may transcend our understanding for the moment, we shall perceive clearly when the day dawns that we no longer see through a glass darkly but then will see face to face.[1]

Read the story of David and Bathsheba found in 2 Samuel 11 and 12. This is the story of a man whose sin led to the loss of his son. He, like us, was the reason the child did not survive. He was also called "a man after God's own heart," a man who understood his own failure and repented of it. This is our story as well. David's God is our God; His promises are our promises. Listen to what the Bible says about seeing your child again someday:

[22] [King] David replied, "I fasted and wept while the child was alive, for I said, 'Perhaps the LORD will be gracious to me and let the child live.' [23] But why should I fast when he is dead? Can I bring him back again? I will go to him one day, but he cannot return to me."

2 Samuel 12:22-23, NLT

[5] Do not be afraid, for I am with you; I will bring your children from the east and gather you from the west. [6] I will say to the north, "Give them up!" and to the south, "Do not hold them back." Bring my sons from afar and my daughters from the ends of the earth—[7] everyone who is called by my name, whom I created for my glory, whom I formed and made."

Isaiah 43:5-7, NIV

Just as David looked forward to being reunited with his son, the day will come when you will see your son or daughter in heaven. There you'll live forever together.

Write Psalm 100:3 on an index card and carry it with you through the week!

Connecting

Flower Ceremony

Your homework assignment last week was to choose and bring to the group meeting a flower or flowers representing your unborn child or children. Why did you choose that particular flower or flowers? Share your reason with others in the group. Place the flowers you brought for your children in the vase provided by your group leader.

If you are not part of a healing group, it is very important to ask your prayer partner to join you in a process of surrendering and releasing your child or children to God this final time. If you are part of a group, be prepared to share this special time with your group members.

Consider these ideas for a personal memorial ceremony:

Prepare an atmosphere of peace and tranquility. Consider using some soft worship music and soft lighting. Spend some time in prayer inviting the Holy Spirit to lead your time saying goodbye to your child. Use this time to express the feelings of a mother's heart for her child, speaking the words you have never been allowed to express openly.

Ask your prayer partner to join you by quietly praying and supporting you during this cherished time. Take the time to imagine that you are holding your child in your arms, maybe speaking his or her name, and identifying some physical traits such as hair color or eye color. Allow the Holy Spirit to guide this process. Each woman experiences exactly and uniquely what God has planned for her during this time of release. You may want to read aloud the letter that you wrote last week or express some new thoughts that come to you. You may ask your prayer partner to share some Scriptures. Trust that God placed this person or group with you for this very special and personal time. He is not only guiding you but will also guide them.

As you continue to imagine holding your child, you will know when it is time to let go. Many women see themselves handing their child to the Lord and experience the peace that comes with letting them go. When you feel ready, close this time in prayer and praise for all God has done through this journey.

TAKING TRUTH HOME

JOURNAL EXERCISE
Use the "Reflections" journal page to capture any thoughts, feelings, or reflections about the memorial service for your child. Allow God to wrap His arms around you this week. If you are not in a group, place your chosen flower in a special vase in your home. Each time you pass it this week, thank God that He holds your child in heaven and He holds you right here on earth!

Review "Who I am" from session 6. Remember that you are a new woman in Christ. God has a plan and purpose for you as a result of all that you have accomplished through this journey.

REQUIRED PROJECT FOR SESSION 8
At the close of our final session, prepare to give each group member (or your prayer partner if you are working through this study on your own) a word of encouragement, a special Scripture verse, or a poem, drawing, bookmark, card, or something else you would like to share. Perhaps there's a certain quality you've admired in a person or something in her spirit that makes her unique. You may be reminded of something a person said to you that lifted you up when you most needed it. This is an opportunity for you to thank your sisters on the journey and acknowledge their contributions to your healing. Take time to personalize your thoughts for each group member.

ONLINE COMMUNITY
Now would be an ideal time to connect with an online community of people on the healing journey from abortions. A Christ-centered online community will give you support and ideas as you continue your healing process. It also gives you an opportunity to positively impact the lives of others on the journey. We strongly encourage you to visit *www.myspace.com/surrenderingthesecret*; *www.surrenderingthesecret.blogspot.com*; or *www.surrenderingthesecret.com* on the Web.

REFLECTIONS

NOTE
1. Adapted from Jack Hayford, *I'll Hold You in Heaven*, (Regal Books, 2003)

PAT'S JOURNAL ENTRY 8

"I am going to open a CPC!" I blurted, breaking into the friendly dinner conversation. Three couples were enjoying dinner with my husband, Mike, and me. All eyes turned my way. "Will you help me, Ann?" I asked.

Precious Ann had walked with me over the past five years of my new Christian life. She was the one who held my hand as I poured out my abortion confession. She was the one who led me straight to her pastor for counsel. Ann was the one who prayed with me as I partnered with several other post-abortive women to form a support group for hurting women hiding out in churches. Ann was my precious friend in Jesus.

"Yes," was her immediate response, followed quickly by, "What is a CPC?"

Sharing my vision to reach out to women in our community with options to abortion, I explained to Ann and our dinner guests about the functions of a Crisis Pregnancy Center.

In early 1988, my husband Mike, my friend Ann, and many others from our church and community began to work, pray, and watch God begin to do wonderful things! For six months we pressed in together to transform my insurance agency into a CPC. God showed up constantly, and we were all convinced that He was totally in control.

Then one morning, just before the center opened, my husband woke up with his own announcement. Instead of his usual, "Good morning," he said, "I want to adopt a little girl." By this time, our sons were 17 and 10. We had been Christians for about 5 years, and I thought I had learned how to be the perfect godly wife. Was I wrong! I'm afraid my response to Mike's announcement was not very submissive. It went something like, "Are you crazy?! Don't you think I have enough on my plate? I have a son who will be a senior in high school, my own insurance business, and I'm trying to start a ministry for God! I am overloaded to the max!"

A long, wonderful story made short ... three months later, we walked into our home with a four-pound baby girl. (God's plans are so much better—so much richer—than mine!) Born to a teenaged birthmother at only 1½ pounds and 10 inches long, she was so beautiful and so perfect. I rocked her and cried with joy for two weeks.

When I walked in to see her for the first time, I was overwhelmed with God's awesomeness. I rounded the corner of the neo-natal intensive care unit and saw her lying on a warmer. In my heart God said, "This, Pat, is what I knit together in a mother's womb. She is My very special creation—My daughter. This is what I have called you to tell others."

SHARE THE JOURNEY

BREAKING THE ICE

1. Use one word to describe yourself when you began this journey with the group. What one word would you use to describe yourself now? Explain the change.

2. As you've reflected this week on the memorial service and your child, what feelings are you processing?

3. Were you able to find some closure through the memorial service? Do you still sense unfinished business with God, others, or yourself? If so, share it with the group.

4. Turn to page 133 and fill in the "Child of My Heart" certificate.

5. As you look ahead, what are your dreams for your future? Name something you've always wanted to do, but have never had the opportunity.

OPENING PRAYER

Jesus, thank You for allowing me to say goodbye to my child ... for now. Today I see myself as I really am—a mother with permission to grieve. No longer am I a captive bound by the secrecy and shame of abortion. I joyfully anticipate my reunion with my little one in heaven, and I am learning to rest in You. I still struggle to understand the depth of Your feelings for me, but I'm thankful for this amazing journey. Help me as I embrace the step that will complete the cycle of my healing process—to help other women be set free!

OBJECTIVES FOR THIS SESSION

- Understand that the healing journey is an ongoing process
- Marvel at what God has for us now and in eternity
- Embrace the vital importance of sharing our stories, both for others and for ourselves
- Realize that God loves to use broken and recovering people in His mission of redemption
- Complete the cycle by finding my unique role in the great adventure

DISCOVERING THE TRUTH

LEADER: *"Discovering the Truth" will help group members to accept and appreciate who they are, while leading them to realize more about who they were created to be and what unimaginable plans God has for them.*

We have traveled an amazing journey together. We are not the same women who came together a couple of months ago. We are not the same women who picked up *Surrendering the Secret*, afraid of what we might find in its pages and afraid to face the truth and pain of the dark secret of abortion. God has been good. He has begun a powerful work of healing in us, and He has brought us to a new time and place. Even though the path ahead is unfamiliar, we're ready to move forward into all He has in store for us.

MY HEALING JOURNEY

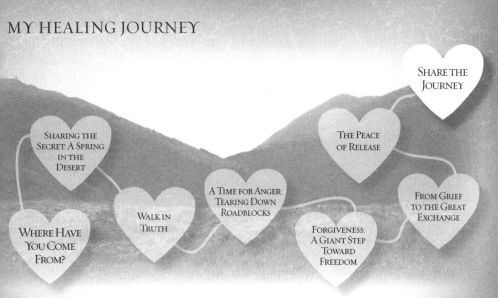

Share the Journey

Sharing the Secret: A Spring in the Desert

The Peace of Release

A Time for Anger: Tearing Down Roadblocks

From Grief to the Great Exchange

Walk in Truth

Where Have You Come From?

Forgiveness: A Giant Step Toward Freedom

YOUR ONGOING JOURNEY

As we close our *Surrendering the Secret* study, please realize that completing the eight steps doesn't mean your journey is completed. It's actually just beginning. This time as a group has been only one chapter in your story.

All the days ordained for me were written in your book before one of them came to be.

PSALM 139:16, NIV

[8] You've kept track of my every toss and turn through the sleepless nights, each tear entered in your ledger, each ache written in your book. … [10] I'm proud to praise God, proud to praise God. [11] Fearless now, I trust in God; what can mere mortals do to me? [12] God, you did everything you promised, and I'm thanking you with all my heart. [13] You pulled me from the brink of death, my feet from the cliff-edge of doom. Now I stroll at leisure with God in the sunlit fields of life.

PSALM 56:8,10-13, THE MESSAGE

1. We've looked at Psalm 139 relative to our children, but these same truths apply to us. Did you realize that God has a book about your life? How does that make you feel? How might it change your approach to life?

2. What do you think is intended by Psalm 139:16, "All the days ordained for me were written in your book"? Have you discovered God's vision for you and the role only you were meant to play?

3. God tracks "every toss and turn" and "each tear" in your life. How does His level of care make you feel? What motivation do Psalm 56 and 139 give you to press on when your journey is difficult?

MORE ...

God is calling you into a great adventure. He has a unique role just for you. As you step outside yourself to engage in the larger story, acknowledge that completing the first pass through the eight steps doesn't mean there's nothing more for you. Here's some of what God has in store for you as you continue the journey with Him:

I [God] will restore the years that the swarming locust has eaten, the crawling locust, the consuming locust, and the chewing locust.

JOEL 2:25, NKJV

Locusts are ravenous, devouring life as they swarm. In this passage, locusts represent the torment or consequences that have come into our lives as a result of bad decisions we or other people have made. In our case, they clearly represent the pain of abortion that has chewed up our lives and relationships.

4. What does God promise in Joel 2:25 that He will do with your life? What degree of restoration does He describe?

[16] I pray that out of his glorious riches he may strengthen you with power through his Spirit in your inner being, [17] so that Christ may dwell in your hearts through faith. And I pray that you, being rooted and established in love, [18] may have power, together with all the saints, to grasp how wide and long and high and deep is the love of Christ, [19] and to know this love that surpasses knowledge—that you may be filled to the measure of all the fullness of God. [20] Now to him who is able to do immeasurably more than all we ask or imagine, according to his power that is at work within us, [21] to him be glory in the church and in Christ Jesus throughout all generations, for ever and ever! Amen.

EPHESIANS 3:16-21, NIV

⁷ We speak of God's secret wisdom, a wisdom that has been hidden and that God destined for our glory before time began. ... ⁹ as it is written: "No eye has seen, no ear has heard, no mind has conceived what God has prepared for those who love him."

I CORINTHIANS 2:7,9, NIV

5. Read carefully through Ephesians 3:16-21 and 1 Corinthians 2:7,9. List all of the incredible things God has for you now and in eternity.

6. How much more do you think God has for you as you continue to merge your story with His story?

THE POWER OF YOUR STORY

God's provisions for the past are not only sufficient, but His promises for our future are incredibly bright! God invites us to become instruments of His love, His life, and His healing power. God has led us on a path to healing; now He wants to use our stories to help others. Our goal now must be to discover and pursue God's purposes for our lives.

Revelation 12:11 shows the power of our stories as it talks about the larger story and the coming final battle between good and evil:

They overcome him by the blood of the Lamb (Jesus), and by the word of their testimony; they did not love their lives so much as to shrink away for death.

REVELATION 12:11, NIV

7. In Revelation 12:11, "they" refers to us—Jesus' followers. "Him" who will be overcome refers to the enemy. What three things are crucial in overcoming the work of the enemy? How can our stories or testimonies be powerful in the battle?

Living Your Story

Remember these three key truths as you pursue your role in the larger story.

KEY 1: God wants us to live for something greater than ourselves!

For everything, absolutely everything, above and below, visible and invisible, rank after rank after rank of angels—everything got started in him and finds its purpose in him.

COLOSSIANS 1:16, THE MESSAGE

I chose you before I formed you in the womb; I set you apart before you were born. I appointed you a prophet to the nations.

JEREMIAH 1:5, HCSB

KEY 2: We are saved to serve God! We are healed to serve others!

⁸ Don't be ashamed of the testimony about our Lord, or of me His prisoner. Instead, share in suffering for the gospel, relying on the power of God, ⁹ who has saved us and called us with a holy calling, not according to our works, but according to His own purpose and grace, which was given to us in Christ Jesus before time began.

2 TIMOTHY 1:8-9, HCSB

¹⁹ Do you not know that your body is a sanctuary of the Holy Spirit who is in you, whom you have from God? You are not your own, ²⁰ for you were bought at a price; therefore glorify God in your body.

1 CORINTHIANS 6:19-20, HCSB

KEY 3: God's power is revealed in our weakness.

²⁶ Brothers, consider your calling: not many are wise from a human perspective, not many powerful, not many of noble birth. ²⁷ Instead, God has chosen the world's foolish things to shame the wise, and God has chosen the world's weak things to shame the strong. ²⁸ God has chosen the world's insignificant and despised things—the things viewed as nothing—so He might bring to nothing the things that are viewed as something, ²⁹ so that no one can boast in His presence. ³⁰ But from Him you are in Christ Jesus, who for us became wisdom from God, as well as righteousness, sanctification, and redemption.

1 CORINTHIANS 1:26-30, HCSB

8. According to 1 Corinthians 1:26-30, what kind of people does God choose to use for His rescue mission in our world? What turns people like us into heroes (verse 30)?

EMBRACING THE TRUTH

LEADER: *"Embracing the Truth" will take group members further down the path to understanding the vital importance of sharing their stories, both for themselves and for others' benefit.*

SETTING HEARTS FREE

As we learn to accept and appreciate who we really are in Him and who He really is in us, God has an adventure waiting for us.

1. Read Isaiah 61:1-3 aloud, replacing "me" with your name.

¹ *The Spirit of the Sovereign* LORD *is on me, because the* LORD *has anointed me to preach good news to the poor. He has sent me to bind up the brokenhearted, to proclaim freedom for the captives and release from darkness for the prisoners,* ² *to proclaim the year of the* LORD's *favor and the day of vengeance of our God, to comfort all who mourn,* ³ *and provide for those who grieve in Zion—to bestow on them a crown of beauty instead of ashes, the oil of gladness instead of mourning, and a garment of praise instead of a spirit of despair.*

ISAIAH 61:1-3, NIV

As you join with Jesus in His mission to bind up the brokenhearted, set captives free, and replace beauty for ashes, you won't believe how exciting and deeply fulfilling that can be!

³ *Blessed be the God and Father of our Lord Jesus Christ, the Father of mercies and the God of all comfort.* ⁴ *He comforts us in all our affliction, so that we may be able to comfort those who are in any kind of affliction, through the comfort we ourselves receive from God.* ⁵ *For as the sufferings of Christ overflow to us, so our comfort overflows through Christ.*

2 CORINTHIANS 1:3-5, HCSB

¹⁴ *But thanks be to God, who always leads us in triumph in Christ, and manifests through us the sweet aroma of the knowledge of Him in every place.* ¹⁵ *For we are a fragrance of Christ to God among those who are being saved and among those who are perishing;* ¹⁶ *to the one an aroma from death to death, to the other an aroma from life to life. And who is adequate for these things?*

2 CORINTHIANS 2:14-16, HCSB

2. How is God the Father portrayed in 2 Corinthians 1:3 and 2:14? How does this portrayal compare to your deepest heart-beliefs about God?

3. How do you think your past wounds and brokenness enhance your usefulness to God in His work of comforting, healing, and setting captives free (2 Corinthians 1:4-5)?

4. What world-changing challenge is placed before us in 2 Corinthians 2:15-16? How would you answer Paul's question: "Who is adequate for these things?"

5. Look again at these two passages from the perspective of what you receive, rather than what you give. What are the benefits to your own recovery and healing as you share with others and become God's "triumph" and "sweet aroma" (2 Corinthians 1:4-5; 2:15-16)?

The amazing thing is that as you work with Jesus in setting captives free, you'll find that one of the captives that's becoming more increasingly liberated is you! God has made some amazing promises to us if we are willing to raise our eyes to Him (above our current pain) and embrace the larger story. These promises give powerful incentive not to give up, but to continue on to still more.

Thousands of women, bound by secret abortions, are sitting in our churches, living as our neighbors, or they may even be our closest friends. Your sharing could help set them free. As Revelation 12:11 illustrates, unmatchable power lies in your willingness to be vulnerable.

NOTE: Using wisdom and prayer to guide your sharing is very important. God will show you how, when, where, and with whom. God would not have you injure or hurt others in the process of sharing.

6. Discuss with your prayer partner or group what cautions you might need to exercise as you begin to share your story with others. Consider your motives, how to wait for God's leading, and other participants in your abortion experience who need healing before you speak out publicly.

7. With whom might you speak privately before sharing your abortion publicly? Your husband? Parents? Do your children know?

8. Brainstorm ways you can use your healing from abortion to reach out to other women who are hurting and still in bondage.

Remember: One great way for you to use your own pain and healing to help others is by joining the online community at *www.myspace.com/surrenderingthesecret* or *www. surrenderingthesecret.blogspot.com.* This is a very private and easy first step to sharing what God has done for you in this healing process. You will also be encouraged and supported by other women as you continue your own journey.

CONNECTING

LEADER: Use this final "Connecting" to launch encourage group members to join Jesus in His work of setting captives free. Make yourself and other group leaders available for ongoing support. Look for ways the group members can continue to support one another. Be sure to celebrate each woman's progress!

Let's Go For It!

Establish some sort of accountability with one another about how you will serve God in helping others as you have been helped. Remember the statistics from session 3 indicated 43 percent of women of childbearing age have been broken by abortion. Only the truth, that you now have, can help set them free.

1. How willing are you to participate in the adventure of setting hearts free? What, if any, reservations do you have?

2. What unique gifts, talents, resources, and life experience has God given you to comfort hurting people, to release them from bondage, or to show them the way to Jesus so they can find redemption from shame and failures?

3. How might people respond to your encouragement that there is a way out of their problems, pain, and destructive behaviors?

4. Continually review session 6 to remind yourself of God's promises to you. Keep God's Word in your mouth and in your heart. Remember, we have decided to *choose life!*

5. Take turns affirming and encouraging each person around the group. This is your opportunity to share with each other a word of encouragement, blessing, special Scripture, poem, drawing, or anything unique you'd like to share with each woman who has taken this journey with you.

My Prayer and Requests and Needs

My Group's Prayer and Requests and Needs

Ideas for the Future

At the end of this Surrendering the Secret experience, those who have been in a group will feel a close sense of connection. At the same time, you're aware that this is the final session. Depending on your own plans for the group and/or the group's views about continuing to meet and study another series, be sensitive to what degree the group needs closure. If members would like to continue studying together, consider the following options ...

OPTION 1: *Continue as a group and study* Redeeming the Tears *(grief and loss),* Radical Reconciliation *(forgiveness),* Beyond the Shadows *(depression),* Stop the Madness *(addictions),* Recovering from Divorce, *or* Great Beginnings.

OPTION 2: *Study* Surrendering the Secret *again, either to go through the process again at a deeper level or to take an active role in helping to lead the group as a mentor, small-group facilitator, or accountability partner. (As the group facilitator, help individuals find their most suitable roles.)*

OPTION 3: *If not enough interested participants want to form a new small group, refer those who are interested to your pastor or staff member to connect them with an ongoing group.*

OPTION 4: *Some support groups like to meet each month or so for a get-together at a restaurant. You may consider offering that as a possibility. Knowing that a reunion is not far off may help many group members with this study's wrap-up, especially if you don't plan to continue meeting as a group.*

Taking Truth Home

Think back to the first time you opened this study. You'll remember that the common thread you have shared with thousands of women was the experience of a past abortion. It is that painful experience that connects you. Thousands more could identify with you as a result of that experience. They need you.

Now that you have completed your journey, you can identify with each other in a new way. You are a group of women bonded by threads of forgiveness, hope, and grace. You are women of courage who have climbed the mountain together, strengthening and encouraging each other every step of the way. You rested when one was weary and linked together as a team to lift one another up. As you persevered together to finish the journey, you gave dignity to your unborn children, tucked them in your heart, and placed them in the arms of Jesus.

Your group's identity is no longer that of post-abortive women. You are women of truth, and your identity is in Christ and who He says you are. You are a new creation in Christ! You are a wounded healer! That abortion that appeared to be a mountain from below is now under your feet. God has been faithful to do what He said He would do. He has set the captives free.

Although you've completed *Surrendering the Secret*, the rest of your life is a continuing journey with Christ. In life, there will always be mountains to climb until you reach your heavenly destination. So, as you go forward, be good to yourself, take time to love yourself, smile inwardly, and keep your sense of humor.

PRAISE TO THE WOMEN ON MY JOURNEY[*]

To the women on my journey
Who showed me the ways to go and the ways not to go.
Whose strength and compassion
Held up a torch and beckoned me to follow.

To the women on my journey
Who showed me how to live and not to live.
Whose grace, success, and gratitude
Lifted me into the fullness of surrender to God.

To the women on my journey
Who showed me what I am and what I am not.
Whose love, encouragement, and confidence
Held me tenderly and nudged me gently ...

To these women I say "Bless You" and "Thank You"
From the depths of my heart, for I have been healed
And set free through your joy and through your sacrifice.

I am grateful for the blessing you have been to me.

— YOUR SISTER IN CHRIST,
Sheri

*Used by permission

Group Meeting Structure

Each group meeting includes five parts.

1. Breaking the Ice

This section includes fun, uplifting questions to warm up the group and help group members get to know one another better as they begin the journey of becoming a connected community. These questions prepare the group for meaningful discussion throughout the session.

2. Discovering the Truth

The heart of each session is the interactive Bible study time. The goal is for the group to discover biblical truths through open, discovery questions that lead to further investigation. The emphasis in this section is twofold: (1) to provide instruction about the process of recovery and freedom; and (2) to understand what the Bible says through interaction within your group.

NOTE: To help the group experience a greater sense of community, it is important for everybody to participate in the "Discovering the Truth" and "Embracing the Truth" discussions. Even though people in a group have differing levels of biblical knowledge, it is vital that group members encourage one another to share what they are observing, thinking, and feeling about the Bible passages.

3. Embracing the Truth

All study should direct group members to action and life change. This section continues the Bible study time, but with an emphasis on leading group members toward integrating into their lives the truths they have discovered. The questions are very practical and application-focused.

4. Connecting

One of the key goals of this study is to lead group members to grow closer to one another as the group develops a sense of community. This section focuses on further application, as well as opportunities for encouraging, supporting, and praying for one another.

5. Taking Truth Home

Between each session, there is some homework for group members. This includes a question to take to God or a question to take to the heart, and typically a journal exercise to help prepare you for the next session. These experiences are a critical part of your journey of healing and freedom.

Supplies and Preparation for Each Session

This section provides an abbreviated list of supplies required for the group experiences and homework in each session of the study. Although not required, a Leader Kit is available and suggested for this study; it includes a member book, a detailed leader guide, and videos for eight sessions on two DVDs (item 005116685).

Session 1: Where Have You Come From?

Supplies: Carabiner for each member and facilitator (available at
www. surrenderingthesecret.com or sporting goods stores)

Preparation:
You may opt to purchase heart-shaped carabiners through *www.surrenderingthesecret.com*.

Homework: Write story, buy journal

Session 2: Sharing the Secret: A Spring in the Desert

Supplies: Journals

Homework: Research; bring drawing, poem, or song

Session 3: Walk in Truth

Supplies: - CD *Pursued by God: Redemptive Worship* from *www.SerendipityHouse.com*
            or bring your own background music
          - CD Player/Audio system
          - TV/DVD system
          - Video *Baby 4-D Sonogram* from *www.SerendipityHouse.com/Downloads.aspx*
          - Tissues

Preparation:
You will lead group members in a short time of listening prayer, in which we invite God to speak into our hearts and lives. Download the free video called *Baby 4-D Sonogram* from *www.SerendipityHouse.com/Downloads.aspx*.

Note:
The *Baby 4-D Sonogram* video will play directly on a computer, on any display screen that connects to your computer, or on some newer DVD systems that play Windows Media

WMV files. However, to play this on most DVD systems requires that you convert this file using DVD authoring software. If you do not have a DVD authoring program on your computer, you may purchase one at a software retailer or online.

Homework: Write anger letters

Session 4: A Time for Anger: Tearing Down Roadblocks

Supplies: - Table for craft project
           - White card stock or heavy paper
           - Frame for collage (optional)
           - Magazines and women's clothing catalogs
           - Scissors, glue sticks, and colored markers

Preparation:
Set up a table with the following materials before the meeting: frames for the final collage (optional); white card stock or heavy paper, several pairs of scissors; magazines, women's clothing catalogs; glue sticks, colored markers. Allow only 10 minutes to create the masks so you have 5 minutes for "show and tell."

Note: This week group members will read their "angry letters."

Homework: Write letter to self and to another woman from God

Session 5: Forgiveness: A Giant Step to Freedom

Option 1 Supplies: - Tub or bucket filled with water
                      - Dissolvo® paper for each group member from a magic supply house or Web site (*www.gospelmagic.com; www.ronjo.com; www.dissolvo.com*—look under creative products)

Option 2 Supplies: - Tub or bucket filled with water
                      - Washable, water-soluble fabric marker for each group member
                      - Scrap of white cloth for each group member

Preparation:
Determine whether Option 1 or 2 works better for you. Try it out before the meeting. Prepare a tub or bucket filled with water. Prepare supplies.

Homework: Foot of the Cross journal entry
LISTENING PRAYER TIME

SESSION 6: FROM GRIEF TO THE GREAT EXCHANGE

Supplies: - See Leader Guide for details

Homework: Letter to child and bring a flower

SESSION 7: THE PEACE OF RELEASE

Note: This is the session for the special memorial service.

Supplies: - Vase for group members' flowers
- Bring flowers as a backup
- Baby doll in a soft blanket

Preparation:
In advance, recruit three volunteers to read parts of the "Who Am I?" list. Set up the vase and have some extra flowers on hand in the event someone isn't able to bring hers. Read through the "Words of Truth" section, and prepare yourself to share it with your group. Recruit a group member in advance to go first in the baby doll experience. Explain the experience to her in advance.

Homework: Bring a note of encouragement, a special Scripture verse, or a poem, drawing, bookmark, card, or something else you would like to share that will encourage each group member.

SESSION 8: SHARE THE JOURNEY

Note:
In this final session, group members share with each other a word of encouragement, special Scripture verse, poem, drawing, or anything unique with each other group member. Be sure to add your own affirmation and encouragement for each woman.

The *Surrendering the Secret Leader Kit* provides one Member Book and one Leader Guide with detailed ideas and step-by-step instructions for each group session along with a video for each session.

For additional ideas and support go to *www.surrenderingthesecret.blogspot.com.*

LEADING A SUCCESSFUL HEALING GROUP

GETTING STARTED

This guide is to help you as a leader to facilitate the *Surrendering the Secret* small-group study. It is recommended that at least one leader has experienced healing from an abortion in her past and has completed the *Surrendering the Secret* study as a participant. It is very acceptable to have another leader who has not had an abortion but who has a passion for helping other women to experience God's healing power and redeeming love. Two leaders are recommended, and a group of four to six participants is ideal.

Ask God to put your group together. Announce the study in your church bulletin, your local crisis pregnancy center, and local women's groups. Set up child care or be certain that group members know that no childcare is provided. Children should not be allowed to attend the sessions. Once started, this will be a closed group and all participants should be pre-enrolled with the leader.

If God has called you to lead a group of women with *Surrendering the Secret*, be ready. Prepare yourself through prayer and fasting. The enemy has worked hard for over 30 years to steal, kill, and destroy (John 10:10) women through abortion. God wants to set them free. This is a tender yet serious undertaking that will bless you as you watch God work in your group members' lives. Enlist prayer support; this will be a spiritual battle.

YOUR MAIN RESPONSIBILITIES AS A GROUP LEADER INCLUDE

- Promoting *Surrendering the Secret* and coordinating enrollment
- Scheduling the group sessions
- Purchasing a *Surrendering the Secret* Leader Kit to enhance your study with video and powerful group experiences.
- Ordering and distributing *Surrendering the Secret* books and other materials
- Securing supplies for facilitated group exercises, specific to each week of the study
- Facilitating each session, using the "Leader" notes included in each session
- Ministering to any group member who may need individual attention during or following a difficult group session

MEETINGS

Surrendering the Secret is designed to be completed over eight weeks, depending on the group's size. Women meet once a week for two hours. Each meeting takes participants step-by-step through the process of post-abortion healing, so consistent attendance is critical. Provide Bibles, pens and pencils, snacks and refreshments, and plenty of tissue.

Each participant will need a *Surrendering the Secret* book which contains the Bible study guide, journal pages, and homework assignments related to each session. Completed homework assignments and journaling are critical to the healing process.

GENERAL TIPS

1. Prepare for each meeting by reviewing the material, praying for each group member, asking the Holy Spirit to join you, and making Jesus the centerpiece of every experience.
2. Create the right environment by making sure chairs are arranged so each person can see the eyes of every other attendee. Set the thermostat to make the room cool. If meeting in a home, make sure pets are in a location where they cannot interrupt. Request that cell phones are turned off unless someone is expecting an emergency call. Have music playing as people arrive (volume low enough for people to converse) and, if possible, burn a sweet-smelling candle.
3. Try to have soft drinks and coffee available for early arrivals.
4. Have someone with the spiritual gift of hospitality ready to make attendees feel welcome.
5. Be sure there is adequate lighting so that everyone can read without straining.
6. Connect with group members away from group time. The amount of participation you'll receive from group members during meetings is directly related to the amount of time that you connect with them away from the meetings.
7. Don't get impatient about the depth of relationship group members are experiencing. Building real Christian community takes time.
8. Provide pens or pencils for attendees at each meeting.
9. Never ask someone to pray aloud without first getting her permission. Ask for volunteers to help with various aspects of the group, including reading aloud.

WHAT CAN YOU EXPECT?

Because group members are experiencing emotions that are still stirring within them, members will be on their best behavior at the outset. Some attendees will, as they understand the openness necessary and requested by the group, withdraw for a time.

Some attendees will experience fatigue that will lead to their shutting down emotionally. This is natural and is one of the things our body does to prevent overload.

There are emotions and phases unique to people dealing with post-abortion trauma. These will be addressed as the group progresses on the healing journey. Be sensitive.

You will be most helpful when you focus on how each individual is adjusting and reminding her that hurt, anger, and other emotions are normal and extremely helpful to understand and express on the path to healing.

When short tempers and changes in physical habits such as sleeping, eating, and apathy appear to be long-term, refer people to a pastor or competent Christian counselor. Ask your pastor or appropriate staff member for help getting a list of quafied counselors.

Places may bring back memories or temptations that are difficult to deal with alone. If a member has an engagement in a location that would be a painful reminder of the past, go with her or ask the group members if one of them might be there for this individual. You may hear, "This is something I have to do alone." You can respect this desire, but remind her that God will give her strength and that you will pray.

What Can You Do?

Support—Provide plenty of time for support among the group members. Encourage members to connect with each other between meetings. Helping each person in the group to develop a strong, supportive accountability group is very important.

Shared Feelings—Reassure the members how normal their feelings are, even if relief and sadness are mixed together. Encourage members to share their feelings with one another.

Advice Giving—Encourage cross-talk (members talking to each other), but limit advice giving. "Should" and "ought to" statements tend to increase the guilt and shame.

Silence—Silence is not a problem. Even though it may seem awkward, silence is just a sign that people are not ready to talk. It DOES NOT mean they aren't thinking or feeling. If the silence needs to be broken, be sure you break it with the desire to move forward.

Prayer—Prayer is vital to healing. Starting and ending with prayer is important. However, people may need prayer in the middle of the session. If a member is sharing and you sense a need to pray, then begin to look for a place to add it.

Feelings vs. Right Choices and Thinking—Group members may be tempted to overemphasize feelings rather than choices and thinking. It is important that you encourage the group to keep moving forward regardless of how they feel. Processing emotions is a vital aspect of the healing journey, but left to feelings alone, progress will shut down.

About the Author

PAT LAYTON is Founder and President of A Woman's Place Ministries, Inc., in Tampa, Florida. A Woman's Place began in 1986 with a healing program for women who have experienced a past abortion. Now called "The Healing Journey," this program formed the basis for the new *Surrendering the Secret* small-group resource for post-abortion healing. The ministry expanded in 1989 to become a Crisis Pregnancy Resource Center offering assistance to women experiencing an unplanned pregnancy. A Woman's Place also offers a full-service abstinence education program called "Impact" that reaches out to young people in the community with facts, fun, and fellowship. Since opening in 1986, A Woman's Place has served over 35,000 women and their families.

Pat is a national speaker and trainer for several national organizations including Care Net, Heartbeat, and the National Council for Adoption. She has produced a daily radio segment, "A Word for Women" and writes articles for newspapers, newsletters, and ministry media, including Focus on the Family and Concerned Women for America. Her personal story was published in *Loved by Choice* by Baker Books in February, 2002.

Pat has numerous awards and honors from peers and state officials as well. She is a member of CARENET (a network of care for women in crisis), CLASS (The Christian Leaders, Authors and Speakers), and the Governor's Media Service Review Team for the Abstinence Education Plan, "Heartbeat"—International Association of Education and Pregnancy Service Providers, the Governor's Partnership for Adoption, and the American Association of Christian Counselors.

Florida Family First honored Pat by giving her the Power of One Award in 1997. In 1999 the Florida State House of Representatives recognized Pat with the Promise of Excellence Award, and in 2000 the Christian Booksellers Association gave her the honor of Best Promotional Materials. Pat keeps busy as a speaker and writer as well as a wife, mother of three, and a very happy grandmother of four. Someday, when life slows down, her secret desire is to write inspirational romance novels. Her determined purpose is to seek and know God more passionately each and every day of her life.

Acknowledgments

My deepest love and gratitude to:

First and most important of all—Father, God, whose mercy, love, and goodness always bring me to my knees.

My amazing husband, Mike—Your support, love, and prayers have carried me and this ministry from behind the scenes for the past 20 years. You are my hero!

My children, Tim, Andy, and Julianna, (and those wonderful daughters-in-law and grands you have added to our nest)—Thank you for allowing me to follow the call of God on my life and for loving me unconditionally along the way.

My *Surrendering the Secret* prayer partner and co-leader, Jayne Solomon—You are my precious friend, my prayer partner, and my encourager. This book would not be in the hands of women who need it if God were not who He is in you!

My Prayer and Writing Team—Jane Masters, Natalie Kane, Judy Call, Kathy Cunningham, Joyce Kelly, Cindy Glover, Pastor Craig Altman, my mom, and my sisters, Pam, Peggy, and Paula.

A Woman's Place Ministries Staff, Board, and Partners—Thank you for 20 years of blessing, victory, support, leadership, and love. Thousands of women have been healed and thousands of babies rescued for life because of your obedience to the call of God.

My Amigos'—It is my very great honor to be a part of such a God-chasing team of ministry leaders. Let's get this to the nations!

The team at Serendipity and LifeWay—You are a wonderful team focused on joining Jesus in His mission to set captives free. Your creative and tireless labor made this life-changing small-group experience a reality.

Managing Director: Ron Keck

Contributing Writer: Ben Colter

Editorial team: Ben Colter, Bethany McShurley, Dale McCleskey, Joyce McGregor, Carolyn Gregory, Melissa Finn, and Nancy Arnold

LifeWay Team: Faith Whatley, Chris Adams, Christa Horton, Maggie Wright, John Kramp, and Dale McCleskey

Cover design Brian Marschall of Marschall Arts,
Interior design and typesetting: Scott Lee of Scott Lee Designs

CHILD OF MY HEART

_____

(child's name here)

MY BEAUTIFUL CHILD, I KNOW YOU ARE SAFE WITH JESUS,

BUT I STILL LONG TO HOLD YOU IN MY ARMS.

YET THAT MUST WAIT UNTIL GOD GATHERS ALL HIS

SONS AND DAUGHTERS FOR THE GLORIOUS REUNION.

I'M SO GLAD WE ARE NOW CONNECTED—YOU AND ME.

UNTIL I CAN HOLD YOU IN MY ARMS,

I WILL HOLD YOU IN MY HEART.

Do not be afraid, for I am with you; I will bring your children from the east and gather you from the west. I will say to the north, "Give them up!" and to the south, "Do not hold them back." Bring my sons from afar and my daughters from the ends of the earth—everyone who is called by my name, whom I created for my glory, whom I formed and made."

ISAIAH 43:5-7, NIV

GROUP DIRECTORY

Write your name on this page. Pass your books around and ask your group members to fill in their names and contact information in each other's books.

Your Name: _____

Name: _____   Name: _____
Address: _____   Address: _____
City: _____   City: _____
Zip Code: _____   Zip Code: _____
Home Phone: _____   Home Phone: _____
Mobile Phone: _____   Mobile Phone: _____
E-mail: _____   E-mail: _____

Name: _____   Name: _____
Address: _____   Address: _____
City: _____   City: _____
Zip Code: _____   Zip Code: _____
Home Phone: _____   Home Phone: _____
Mobile Phone: _____   Mobile Phone: _____
E-mail: _____   E-mail: _____

Name: _____   Name: _____
Address: _____   Address: _____
City: _____   City: _____
Zip Code: _____   Zip Code: _____
Home Phone: _____   Home Phone: _____
Mobile Phone: _____   Mobile Phone: _____
E-mail: _____   E-mail: _____

Name: _____   Name: _____
Address: _____   Address: _____
City: _____   City: _____
Zip Code: _____   Zip Code: _____
Home Phone: _____   Home Phone: _____
Mobile Phone: _____   Mobile Phone: _____
E-mail: _____   E-mail: _____

Name: _____   Name: _____
Address: _____   Address: _____
City: _____   City: _____
Zip Code: _____   Zip Code: _____
Home Phone: _____   Home Phone: _____
Mobile Phone: _____   Mobile Phone: _____
E-mail: _____   E-mail: _____

JOURNAL

JOURNAL

JOURNAL

JOURNAL

JOURNAL

Journal

JOURNAL

Journal

JOURNAL

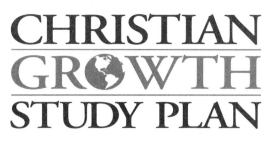

CHRISTIAN GR🌐WTH STUDY PLAN

In the Christian Growth Study Plan *Surrendering the Secret* is a resource for course credit in the subject area Prayer in the Christian Growth category of diploma plans. To receive credit, read the book; complete the learning activities; attend group sessions; show your work to your pastor, a staff member, or a church leader; then complete the form. This page may be duplicated. Send the completed form to:

Christian Growth Study Plan
One LifeWay Plaza; Nashville, TN 37234-011
fax (615) 251-5067; e-mail *cgspnet@lifeway.com*
For information about the Christian Growth Study Plan, refer to the current *Christian Growth Study Plan Catalog*, located online at *www.lifeway.com/cgsp*. If you do not have access to the Intern contact the Christian Growth Study Plan offic (800) 968-5519, for the specific plan you need

Surrendering the Secret: The Healing Journey to Post-Abortion Recovery
COURSE NUMBER: CG–1322

PARTICIPANT INFORMATION

Social Security Number (USA ONLY-optional)	Personal CGSP Number*	Date of Birth (MONTH, DAY, YEAR)
- -	-	- -

Name (First, Middle, Last)		Home Phone
		- -

Address (Street, Route, or P.O. Box)	City, State, or Province	Zip/Postal Code

Email Address for CGSP use

Please check appropriate box: ❑ Resource purchased by church ❑ Resource purchased by self ❑ Other

CHURCH INFORMATION

Church Name

Address (Street, Route, or P.O. Box)	City, State, or Province	Zip/Postal Code

CHANGE REQUEST ONLY

☐ Former Name

☐ Former Address	City, State, or Province	Zip/Postal Code

☐ Former Church	City, State, or Province	Zip/Postal Code

Signature of Pastor, Conference Leader, or Other Church Leader	Date

*New participants are requested but not required to give SS# and date of birth. Existing participants, please give CGSP# when using SS# for the first time. Revise
Thereafter, only one ID# is required. **Mail to:** Christian Growth Study Plan, One LifeWay Plaza, Nashville, TN 37234-0117. Fax: (615)251-5067.